The Autobiography of James Graves (a personal record)

James Graves (1833 - 1911)

Copyright © 2016 Dosanda Publications

Cover design & cover text © 2016 Donard de Cogan
Editors' Foreword © 2016 Anne de Cogan
Editors' Footnotes © 2016 Donard & Anne de Cogan

All rights reserved in all media. No part of this book may be used or reproduced without written permission, except in the case of brief quotations embodied in critical articles and reviews

Published in the United Kingdom 2016 by Dosanda Publications

ISBN 978-0-9935469-2-1

Editors' Foreword

This is a very Victorian rags-to-riches story.

James Graves was born in 1833. He was the second son of John Graves, a poor farm worker from Cottenham, rural Cambridgeshire. John was a serious and studious man who, despite having very little formal education, eventually became a schoolmaster in Bedfordshire and later in Kent. James had the benefit of attending primary school, where he was particularly good at arithmetic and even asked a local cleric to help him learn the elements of algebra. His father was very supportive of his efforts, and while still children themselves, James and his elder brother helped out with free evening classes for the farm children of the neighbourhood.

Unlike his brother, James did not become a registered schoolmaster. At the age of fourteen he saw his first telegraph poles running alongside a railway line, and was fascinated by this new technology. Whether or not this was what led him to seek a job as clerk with the Electric Telegraph Co six years later, this appointment took his life in a decisive new direction.

His first posting was in Southampton, where he proved to be a diligent worker, and was soon promoted to Clerk-in-Charge at the Jersey cable station, where he remained for 3 years. By this time he was married to his childhood sweetheart, with a young family. He left Jersey in 1861 to take up a position as engineer on the the Company's cable repair ship, Monarch, before becoming superintendent of the new cable station in Valentia where he remained in charge for 43 years.

This autobiography finishes at the end of the Jersey period. It is very probable that he intended to write a second volume, but his work and family commitments were becoming more onerous and time must have been at a premium. He did leave behind a "technical autobiography" devoted to cable engineering and a short curriculum vitae which was probably intended to show off his handwriting when he applied for his first temporary clerical post as a teenager.

The editors are very grateful to the late Robbie Graves, great grandson of James, for entrusting them with bringing this document to public notice, and to Dominic de Cogan for patiently and painstakingly transcribing it.

The author in old age with his son, grandson and great-grandson

Note

We have attempted to edit this document as lightly as possible, using James Graves' own writing style except where doing so would cause confusion to a modern reader. Footnotes, photographs and some extracts from his other writings have been added for interest. Graves makes extensive use of dashes and the equal sign as punctuation marks. The equals sign is still used by radio amateurs as an alternative to a full stop.

Introduction

In penning the following pages, if they should ever chance to be published to the world after I shall be no more, I wish to present to my readers a clear, concise and true account of the different circumstances which have taken place with immediate reference to myself since I was by the providence of God brought into this world of sorrow and affliction; and if what I shall relate, may be in any way interesting to those whose eyes it shall by any chance meet and shall help to pass away a few leisure moments in an amusing, innocent and instructive manner, I shall consider myself fully repaid for the time and trouble, which I may from time to time in my leisure hours devote in the production of this little work.

Chapter the 1st

Without prolonging my readers' anxiety to commence the leading facts of what the title of this work would lead them to suppose it contains - I will proceed to give an explanation of the title of the book as some of my readers may perhaps say "what is an autobiography? This is a strange word and we don't know what it means - can anyone tell us what is meant by an autobiography?" Now in case these should not be within the reach of an English Dictionary, on, in case they have no one to enlighten their minds upon the subject, I will, before I proceed further just explain the title of my work. An 'autobiography' then is the life of a person written by himself or herself as the case may be, therefore the title of this little work would intimate that the reader may expect throughout the following pages an account of the different incidents worthy of notice that have occurred during the life of that person whose biography is herein detailed by himself, this for the instruction of the humbler classes of my readers who might not hitherto have exactly understood the term made use of in the title. I am sure that those of my readers who have received a far more liberal education than the class I have alluded to above, will pardon my seeming simplicity in explaining the word when I state that having, as will be seen from the following pages, been so accustomed to the intercourse of the humbler classes of society and their children, I have observed a very great laxity in their education and especially with respect to what they term "long hard words". They cannot seem to comprehend the meaning of the terms made use of in many works; therefore it is necessary, in bringing a work before the public for the instruction of all grades of society, to make use of such words as will be equally understood by the humbler classes of society and those of more superior education; to the latter of who, having their minds more enlarged and enlightened, the explanation I have given of the word 'autobiography' is naturally needless, but from the reasons I have advanced, I trust that my more enlightened readers will perceive my subject, and, in sympathising with those of less intelligence, will pardon my intrusion so long upon this subject. Resting assured that they will do so, I proceed to give as concise an autobiography of myself as I possibly can, endeavouring at the same time to make it as amusing and instructive as I can and thereby rendering it interesting to all classes of my readers, whether learned or ignorant, high or low, rich or poor, master or servant, husband or wife, boy or girl, in fine, to all into whose hands it may chance to fall, that they may be enabled to see how I worked my way through the world and if they approve of my course, they may endeavour to adopt it, if not too late and by so doing endeavour to obtain the blessings that I have done by the assistance, guidance and bountiful goodness of the Almighty.

Chapter 2nd

The large and populous village of Cottenham, situate about seven miles from the town of Cambridge – that seat of learning, which sends forth to all parts of the world from its university, men of sound knowledge, wisdom and scientific skill – may be found the spot where the family name of Graves has for a long series of years been very familiar. I will not trace my genealogy further back than my grandfather, Thomas Graves, who lived to the grand old age of 68 years and died on the 25th day of October 1840 in the above village where his remains now lie waiting the sound of the trumpet of the archangel which shall awake the dead. He was a very pious, hardworking and industrious man – he parted this world in peace and his death was lamented by all his friends and relatives. His wife, Ann Graves, my grandmother, was likeminded with her husband, of a sincere and christian spirit- after living to the age of 79 years she was summoned to render up her account on the 8th day of February 1854. Her death was as much lamented as her husband's had been.

The location of Cottenham in relation to Cambridge. The distance is about 9 miles

My Father, John Graves, son of the above-mentioned Thomas and Ann Graves, was born on the 17th of September 1807. He was taken from school at the age of ten years in order to work to earn a small income to add to that of his parents who were in humble circumstances of life. He worked for some time in a brick-field and afterwards he changed his employment for farming:- this was more healthy and more suitable to his taste and constitution. Once during his employment in this line he fell from the top of a load of hay and providentially escaped with slight injury − at another time whilst he was milking a cow, the animal became restless and trode on his ankle, which was sprained and caused him much pain. Once in the harvest field a severe test was put to his temperate habits. He with several others were having their luncheon in the field and they wanted to compel him to drink more that he felt inclined to do, knowing himself that he had had sufficient − they then threatened to throw it all over him if he did not drink it − he told them in very, very cool but emphatic terms to do so, for he would not drink more that was sufficient for him. They accordingly poured the contents of the pot over him which he choose rather than to drink it. There are not many who would have stood so severe a test in a hot harvest field, but it proved that he had good moral courage and self-denial, which qualities, I firmly believe assisted him as much as his abilities in prosecuting his after career. He had during his few school days made the best use of his time and so completely surprised his master by his aptness and rapid progress that in a short time he could work out almost any problem in simple arithmetic (his favourite study) and his master seeing this, on his arrival through the applicational rules of the first four of arithmetic passed him over the intermediate rules thinking to puzzle him to the vulgar and decimal fractions and more complicated rules, but nothing daunted - my Father went to his study with a full determination to conquer and he succeeded:- His master at length found he could not puzzle him in arithmetic at all. In writing he made some progress but not equal in proportion to that in arithmetic and his succeeding hard work well might have spoiled his style of writing. After a few years he went apprentice to a boot and shoe maker at Cambridge. During the interval between his leaving school and his going apprentice, he attended, as often as circumstances would permit, an evening school, and thus kept fresh in his mind his little stock of knowledge which he was constantly increasing by observation and experience, until by dint of great perseverance he succeeded in making himself a tolerable scholar in general subjects in the old-fashioned style of education – for schools, systems, subjects and methods of study have so wonderfully altered since then, that a person who was then considered well educated would now-a-days, with the same amount of education and intelligence be considered a very ignorant man:- all that was thought sufficient for an education was to be able to read and write and to know how to work out a few common problems in arithmetic sufficient to keep, in their way, a set of books in an office, and to manage to make out a Debtor and Creditor account. What a vast field of labour has since been cultivated! When we compare the present state of education with what it was and contemplate what has already been done, we cannot but thank Him, who in His allwise and all merciful Providence, has thus extended to us, his sinful creatures, the blessings of wisdom, science and education in all their respective branches! And also praise Him that he has laid open before us the vast Book of Nature, from which we may, day after day and every day, glean something fresh, amusing and instructive, and which will lead our thoughts from worldly things to heavenly things:- we are hereby prompted to sincerely thank him again and again for his great and unbounded wisdom and goodness in thus extending His favours to us his unworthy sinful creatures – and in contemplating these His mercies we are urged to set our affections on things above and not on things on the earth.

But to return to my subject:- my Father fulfilled the terms of his apprenticeship and set up in business for himself, his principal customers were the gentry and the collegians, he soon became respected and his fame as being a first rate workman soon got abroad- he obtained good trade and was universally respected by the "town and gown". At length he became acquainted with a young woman by the name of Sarah Tofts who was at that time living in service with the Revd. George Adam Brown the clergyman at Chesterton, a pretty little village lying on the opposite bank of the river Cam from Cambridge at a distance of nearly 3 miles from the town. During the time that Miss Tofts was in the service of the above gentleman, she experienced numerous dangers and severe trials of her courage. As her master frequently visited the college at Cambridge and having a bed there he would oftentimes stay there all night and on such occasions, she, being the only servant in the house was left alone in a very large mansion situate in the centre of a large garden apart form the village. On one of these occasions, she had been out with her "amant" and it was getting very late:- he accordingly accompanied her home and it was determined he should sleep in the house that night, which would render it more safe:- during the night a noise was heard of a window being thrown open (the drawing room windows opened upon the lawn by being thrown upwards through the ceiling)- she heard it – struck a light- her "amant" had heard it too and also obtained a light. Sarah ran to his room quietly and called him- he was ready – they proceeded to the top of the house and rang the alarm bell very violently, at the sound of which footsteps were heard to proceed along the pathway through the garden. They then went and searched every room they came to, up the chimney, in the closets, under the tables, in fact everywhere in which a man might conceal himself. At last they came to the drawing room when they saw that the large window thrown up and left open, scarcely a thing touched and no one near:- it was evident they had providentially heard the first sounds and having immediately given the "alarm" the villain thought it best to make his escape "sans ceremonie". The grounds being moist the footprints of the burglar were plainly visible:- The dimensions, marks of the nails and every other particular were taken by her "amant" in the morning. It was plainly evident that he the intruder whom he might be was a person who knew the ground, the house and the gates well. The key of the great iron gates at the entrance was always kept in a niche in the wall covered with ivy, known only to those connected with the house. It was firmly believed and was the expressed opinion of all inhabitants that the burglar was no other than a Frederick Roe who was formerly and until within a few weeks of this occurrence, the gardener of the Revd. Gentleman and was consequently well acquainted with every quarter of the garden and also with every room in the house, this together with the size of the footprints and the marks exactly corresponding with a pair of boots which he was well known to have in his possession, confirmed the general opinion that he was the burglar and undoubtedly would have been the assassin had he not been so unexpectedly deterred from prosecuting his villainous intentions- but in the absence of any witness or proof of his guilt, as no one saw him, the vile wretch escaped the punishment of the law and he left the country for some years, thereby substantiating his guilt. Had it not been most providentially ordered that she had a man sleeping in the house that night, she would in all probability have been murdered by the villain and the house plundered, but thanks be to God she was preserved and the property left undiminished! How then could she express her gratitude to him who had by God's providence been the instrument in His hands in saving her life – otherwise than by loving him (whom she already loved) with an increased and never dying affection? A short time after on the 27th day of March 1831 they were married at Chesterton by the Revd G.A. Brown, her old beloved master, whose eyes were filled with tears while performing that service which would separate him from a faithful, trustworthy and affectionate servant who had served him during eleven long years, and which would join her in hand and heart to the object of her love and affection whom she there promised to love, to cherish and to obey. Thus parted she from her old master who promised that he would not forget the services she had done him during her long residence with him. There is every reason to believe that the poor old gentleman kept his promise, but which the world, the covetousness of which increases ever more and more deprived her of. It was stated in his will, made at the time that she and another female servant were living with him, that he "willed and bequeathed" a certain sum of money etc "to each of his two servants", but it failed to state the names of these "two servants" and upon his death, the two servants then living with him claimed the amount and other properties, which unquestionably were intended by the deceased to come to her and the other servant who were living with him at the time the will was made. There being no names mentioned however, it could not be disputed and thus it was that his poor, faithful and affectionate servant was deprived of that which she was undoubtedly entitled to, but such is life! such is the world, ever covetous – ever scrambling for riches whether right or wrong – ever like the horse leech crying "give, give" and never satisfied – those who have most get more and become domineering and those who have little, yea even though they be the rightful owners, get cheated, trampled upon and robbed! But although thus robbed of a little fortune which would have made her and her's comfortable for a long time, yet thank God she had by God's grace and the exertions of her husband been hitherto enabled to gain an honest livelihood and pay every man twenty shillings in the pound.

After they had been married about 9 or 10 months, during which time they lived in a state of blessed harmony, they were blessed on the 15th day of January 1832 with a firstborn son, who was born at Chesterton and christened after the name of his father and that of his mother's brother, James*:- and about one year and seven months after that, viz on the 4th August 1833 – their second son was born in the same place and christened by the name of "James". This son, James, is the humble author of this book, of whom his readers will hear more in the ensuing chapters.

---

* It is with great pleasure that I am enabled to state that at the time I write this – September 1855 – my Brother John James Graves is and has been for the last four years comfortably situated as master of an Endowed Charity School at Lamport, Northamptonshire. He is married and has one son – He is an excellent Scholar and Teacher.

Chapter 3rd

Soon after and while I was an infant my parents removed with their little charges to Cambridge and when I was about four years of age I was sent to an infant school conducted by a Mrs Eaton who taught me the first principles of reading and when a little older I was removed to another infant school under the management of a Mrs Hazlewood from whom I learned those elementary principles of education which are generally taught in infant schools including tables, spelling, reading and very simple arithmetic. While in this school I well remember a prize – a very pretty hymn book with gilt edges – being offered to that child who on the following week say the Ten Commandments the most perfectly. I seemed to have an anxious desire to obtain it and strove with all my energies to do so. The following week came and brought with it the examination day and amongst the different scholars I stood up as a competitor for the prize. The examination concluded, I was declared the conqueror and was accordingly presented with the book, which I have possessed to this day and value it much, it being the first prize that I had obtained and that too for learning the ten commandments, this much have been about the year 1839 = In the following year I was transferred from the Infant School to the Boys National School, having arrived at the age of 7 years at which age it was usual to transfer scholars from one school to the other being under the same jurisdiction as each other = The National School was a large room and well filled with children from 150 to 200 generally being present, it was conducted by Mr Newland, a man of great severity, strict order and discipline being his system:- he was a man of tolerable experience as a Schoolmaster, well proportioned, not very tall, but rather strong-built, dark hair and a look of piercing sternness when angry, but very mild in his manner when in a good temper, a very fair writer and arithmetician, 'enfin' a tolerably well-educated man of his class and standing in society. I was entered in the eighth or lowest class but very soon left that for the seventh and so on upwards, until I found myself in June 1844 to have been some months in the second class. About the year 1843 Mr Hullah opened a singing class which was continued by his assistant Mr Bannister in the King Street School and an order was sent to our school for a few of those scholars who appeared to have the best ears for music and whose general conduct would warrant their being received as free privileged scholars. I was chosen amongst the number and having already a slight knowledge of music I found the exercises came easy to me and thus many a long evening was passed very comfortably, instructively and entertainingly. I continued to receive these lessons up to the time of our exodus from Cambridge of which more hereafter. It may be remarked, perhaps, that I must have possessed very extraordinary talents, or some other means of instruction other than that received during school hours in order to raise me from the lowest to the second class in the short space of about three years – while others of the scholars oftentimes remained a year or more in one class without making one step upwards. I will inform my readers how it was- I have already remarked that my father possessed a tolerable education gained during his few school days, but more especially by self-application and hard study afterwards- this he employed in the advancement of his children's education; for while at his work, he would have my older brother one side of him and me on the other and give us examples in arithmetic and other questions to answer- and there we sat, working one against the other, our father giving us every necessary instruction we might require and explaining to the best of his abilities what we did not understand; thus, we were always kept at home more advanced than at school, so that by this means if we were put into the fifth rule at school we were always prepared for it and never puzzled over it, having done the puzzling work already at home. Thanks be to my father for thus forwarding my education and keeping me regularly at school where I received the basic and solid foundation upon which my after study rested, and having laid a good foundation the other subjects that were afterwards build upon it stand firm as on a rock and will never be forgotten by me as long as I shall live. Would that all parents who are able would endeavour to forward their children's education at home! How many unnecessary corrections would be spared the child, how many words and long explanations would be saved the school teacher and how much more would be learned by young people during their school days? The bud of youth at that time is bursting forth and with it the bud of knowledge:- then is the time for learning when the mind is young and anxious, thirsting as it were after knowledge and as it expands it must be kept filled – no vacuum can exist in the mind of either manhood or youth or childhood, it must be filled with good or bad, the mind of childhood catches at everything presented to its vision to fill up the expanding space = how important then, is it, that good principles and sound educational subjects should be prepared to place before it, that it may while its appetite for subject matter is keen and while the seed must be sown for the future good of the child, or for contrary, be enabled to imbibe those principles which will grow up in it and bring forth much and good fruit. How necessary is it also for parents at home to instil into the minds of their children religious principles while the mind is yet young, tender and capable of being trained – without which they cannot truly prosper through life, or even if they should do, what the world calls "prosper" – what shall it avail them if they "gain the whole world and loose their souls"? I would therefore again urge all parents to train up their children in habits of piety and at the same time not to forget their secular education – but above all give them Christian principles that like Timothy they may be taught betimes to know God's holy word that they may grow up in the nurture and admonition of the law and that as they grow in wisdom and stature, they may also grow in favour with God and man. Oh! Parents, Guardians and all who have the care of children, do take notice of this appeal, as coming from one who has known and does know – who has experienced and does experience and hopes ever to experience the inexpressible and incalculable benefits that are to be derived from an early Christian and religious and at the same time a liberal secular education:- do, I beseech you, listen to the advice of one who knows the benefit of it and give your children and those committed to your charge a liberal education, both religious and secular – no one can tell the blessings to be derived from these but those who have experienced them, and where will find a single person who has a good education, who would be willing, were it possible , to sell it to anyone, and at what price would he offer it, if such could be found? For all the gold in the country? No – for wisdom is more valuable than gold – Oh then give your children "That wisdom for which gold shall not be paid and for which silver neither shall be weighed".

5 Eden Street Cambridge where the Graves family lived and worked

On the 9th day of August 1843 about 3.0pm the clouds began to gather over very dismally and showed evident signs of an approaching storm. Our schoolmaster dispatched us all home almost immediately and the scholars who lived a great distance could scarcely have arrived home before a most terrific storm centred itself over the town and the thunder lightning hail and rain which followed were of the most awful description. No one in the town remembered such a storm. Greenhouses, churches, colleges, dwelling houses of all descriptions and in fact every piece of exposed glass was smashed to atoms, the forked lightning which rent the heavens was of the most terrific nature = The inhabitants of Cambridge, even the very worst of reprobates, were many of them found to be praying, for they thought that the world was at an end. The hailstones – if such they could be called- were as large as hen's eggs – large lumps of ice of all shapes and sizes. After the storm was over, I and my Brother went round the town and one of the most distressing sights presented itself = the town looked from one end to the other as if it had been besieged by some enemy, scarcely a window could be seen whole, nor scarcely a pane of glass = and on an estimate being made, it was found that there was not more than one third sufficient glass in the Kingdom to repair the damage done by this storm in Cambridge alone = Cellars were filled with rain and hail, houses flooded, drains broken up, trees, plants and flowers of all descriptions entirely demolished, the corn not yet in was thrashed in the fields. Several people fainted away of fright, one woman who lived next door to us, but who had come into our house at its commencement, fainted away and was with great exertions restored again. This storm will never be forgotten by anyone who was of sufficient age to remember the circumstance for it left an impression upon the minds of the inhabitants which will not be very easily eradicated. It was a great providence that our master, Mr John Newland, sent the scholars home early that afternoon, apprehending a storm, or we should have just left school at the time of its commencement, which took place a little after 4.0pm. I shall never forget that storm as long as I live.

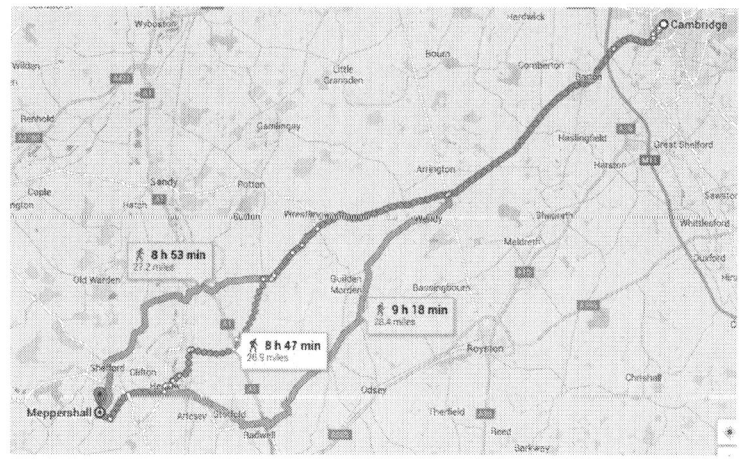

The walking route from Cambridge to Meppershall

Chapter 4th

On the sixth day of June 1844 – my father's trade not suiting his health and constitution, he applied for and obtained the mastership of a small school at Meppershall Bedfordshire – we left our home at Cambridge and proceeded on our way about seven o'clock in the morning, having a journey of 32 miles – cross country before us. We had got about 10 or 11 miles on our way when it was found impossible to proceed further with the horse with which we had started, he having turned jib soon after we left Cambridge and with difficulty we had managed to traverse the above distance, it was therefore imperatively necessary to obtain another horse, which we did after some little difficulty and bargaining. We took out the jib and left him behind and started off again with a much younger, but good strong horse and reached our destination in safety at dusk. We unloaded and put the horse in a stable and the cart into the yard of a farmer who was kind enough to offer us the same voluntarily. The man slept in the house and was up again at daylight to retrace his steps back to Cambridge. We wished him a pleasant journey and he left us. We were very busy that and the following day arranging our goods and chattels in order. Having got a little comfortable we proceeded to Meppershall to look at the place etc. It must be understood that the village of Meppershall and the school were 1 1/2 mile apart from where we were obliged to live, namely at Shillington, there not being a suitable house for us in the former village. We found Meppershall, or Mepsal to be situated very pleasantly about 8 miles from Hitchen – 3 miles from Shefford and 12 miles from Bedford; it lies in an angle between Hitchen and Shefford – these two towns being 7 miles apart and Mepsal lying about 2 miles off the W side of the high road from about 1 1/4 mile from Shefford, thus forming the apex of an obtuse angled triangle.

> In his concise autobiography the author describes Meppershall as
>
> " a small Agricultural Parish, small with regard to the number of inhabitants, but large in extent, it abounds with meadows, cornfields and woods, hills & valley are in abundance, the inhabitants are of a generally mild and obliging disposition, this being a plaitting county, the females and a great number of the

male population, tog? with the children are employed in making straw plait for bonnets, scarcely a house in the place can be found where there is no plait made, Some of the females are wonderfully expeditious at making it, making sometimes from 30 to 40 yards a day; there are schools for plaitting where the children go some to be taught but most of them to sit and work together, as many of them can do it without looking at their work, they can converse with each other or read at the same time that they are at work, but a great part of their time is passed away by conversation or by singing and repeating some little rhymes they have learnt from others. A favourite one is the following which explains the manner of making the seven straw plait which is the commonest sort and the most made

>Under one and over two
>Pull it tight and that will do

The younger children soon learn these lines and which they find helps them to learn very much; indeed, it is a constant rule in their minds by which they are to do their work; the plait is taken to Shefford a market town 3 miles distant every Friday where the plait buyers are ready to buy it from them. Friday is the market day for other things as well.

Women plaiting by lamplight

This village is in two counties the boundary line of Beds and Herts passing across it and thro' the old Lordship House, in which we resided during the latter part of our stay there: this is an ancient old house and on a beam across the middle of the ceiling of one of the largest rooms is a plate with this inscription-

>If you wish to go into Hertfordshire
>Hitch a little nearer to the fire"

[Eds]

The country round here is very pleasant indeed, there being some splendid views from almost very quarter. The churchyard at Meppershall is calculated as being the highest point in Bedfordshire, the bottom of the chancel door of the church being exactly level with the top of the spire of Shillington church which stands on a hill raised above the houses in the town, so much so that the floor of the church is several feet higher than many of the chimneys of the high house. Therefore some idea may be formed of the altitude of Meppershall in comparison with the surrounding country, thus rendering it extremely healthy and the air of a pure, light and refreshing nature; longevity is not at all uncommon here.

> In Meppershall Parish Register [P29/1/8] Rev. J.H. Howlett records that "In 1839 the Rev[eren]d Henry Howarth, then Rector of this Parish, granted a part of the Orchard belonging to the Glebe as a site for a National School Room, which was erected at a cost of one hundred and forty pounds from Her Majesty's Treasury, a grant of ten pounds from the National Society, a grant of fifteen pounds from the Bedfordshire Board of Education, and voluntary subscriptions". [Eds]

The Schoolroom was a neat little building, newly built being the first school ever erected in the Parish:- the inhabitants were not very numerous but the parish was very extensive and the few houses were scattered about very much all over it, here and there one, the people from the cause I have just named of there never having been a school there before, we found to be very ignorant. However, my father opened the school with the assistance of the Rector (the Revd H. Howarth − now (1855) Rector of St George Hanover Square London, my eldest brother and myself − but it was long before any visible change took place they were so void of understanding and so uncultivated that it seemed almost impossible to make them understand anything, however, after a time and by Gods Blessing on our labour we began to see that our seed was not sown in 'vain' but that "after many days" we saw the transformation begin to take place and a change for the better was becoming visible, not only to us but also to the parents of the children and their elder brothers and sisters, who seeing their younger children and brothers and sisters begin to read and write and talk about what they had heard at <u>school</u>, a word scarcely known to them before we went there, they also expressed an anxious desire to learn, but being too fully occupied at their work during the day they could not attend day school, so desired us to open them an evening school in the winter months and it was agreed upon that as soon as the days got shorter and long evenings commenced we were to open an evening school – thus the matter rested. Before this winter commenced we were compelled to quit the house we occupied at Shillington as the farmer to whom it belonged required it for his own use and there still being no suitable house in the village we were compelled to remove to the nearest one we could find empty, which we found to be alongside the high road from Bedford to London – between Shefford and Hitchen and a quarter of a mile from the former of these two thus giving us 3 miles walk to School every morning – the consequence was that one of us (my elder brother and I) had to stay at home in the morning in turns to take dinner to the School, this was done every day except when we took cold dinner with us in the morning. While living here being so near the post town for letters – the nearest to Meppershall and the adjacent villages, my brother and I undertook to act as post boys for the villages round about – the proceeds of this went to find ourselves in clothes, the deliver of the letters took up generally nearly all the morning on account of the distances to be walked:- One snowy morning I managed to loose the footpath on a grass field road called the "baulk" and there being a ditch on either side, both filled level with the road with snow, I had the misfortune to walk into the right hand ditch, up to my neck in snow. I extricated myself as quickly as possible and found that I had received no damage save a "cooling", not being very comfortable in cold weather. The winter of 1845 having arrived Father and I resolved upon opening an evening school according to our promise (my elder Brother had left home and was in a situation in London as assistant master at St Ann's National School). The youths and maidens of the village were delighted at such a chance to learn and thankful that, at last, some means of education had been placed within their reach, and they eagerly embraced this opportunity of making a commencement. Thanks be to God that by his gracious providence and assistance, our endeavours to impart, and theirs to imbibe useful knowledge brought about most satisfactory results. By the end of the winter they had all made extraordinary progress in the different branches of education they had been taught, but especially in reading, writing and cyphering:- many, who could not read at all, and some who knew not the alphabet when we commenced, were now able to read a chapter of Holy Writ with tolerable ease and correctness, some could work out a simple, and others a more complicated, problem in arithmetic and spell with tolerable correctness. In their writing they had made very good progress and most of them bid fair to become good writers, but seasons cannot last longer than their appointed length of time − neither is it right that they should, so the winter gradually wore away and the evenings became shorter, the light lasting longer and the occupations of our scholars calling them in the fields and other places − we were, much to the regret of ourselves and our scholars, compelled to give up our evening school until the following winter, which was anxiously looked forward to by those whose appetite for knowledge was still keen, and, who were longing for more of our wholesome useful food, in both religious and secular instruction. Thus ended, and such were the results of our first winter's evening school in this poor ignorant and neglected village! We will now take leave of the evening scholars for a few months and leaving them to get in their harvest and other summer occupations: we will revert to another subject, but before I entirely quit the subject of this winter's evening school I will relate one little anecdote of myself which occurred during the time and consequent upon the key of this school. Our custom was on locking up the school, to take the keys to the Rectory, about 3 minutes walk from the school, through a large orchard in which were two large fishponds, or moats, one beside the pathway and the other forming two sides of a square running along the side and back of a kitchen garden = formerly this moat extended completely round the whole ground and the house in the centre was approached by means of a drawbridge − which was removed at night thus rendering the house secure from intruders − within this enclosure stood the house − the back premises − the flower and kitchen garden, a shrubbery and in front of the house a carriage drive, and on the main side in which were the principal windows there was a very fine and beautifully set grass lawn at either end an immense yew tree − one side (the right) was ended by a very tall yew hedge – the centre open railings – and on the left a boarded fence enclosing the kitchen garden – some rose trees and other creeping vines ornamented the blank spaces between the windows reaching nearly to the eaves – the house surrounded by a fine gravelled path leading one way to the garden and the other, to the village, via the carriage drive. From these particulars some faint idea may be formed of the house and its situation and it may naturally be inferred that it presented altogether a most pleasing and delightful aspect and was very high. One very dark night – so dark that the ground could not be seen, not the path distinguished except for its roughness, in comparison to the grass underfoot, I had a very narrow escape of my life. I was proceeding just before my father back through the orchard having left the school keys at the Rectory, when having reached within a couple of yards of the border of the moat running beside the path my father called "stop". I, not knowing where I was, nor what was the matter stood motionless – "You are on the edge of the moat" he resumed "turn back towards me or you will be in it" I followed the sound of his voice and found him, when I learned, he could see my shadow on the lightness of the water which, however dark generally shows a little brightness, but which I had not perceived, however, he could discern my figure approaching in the direction of the water and stopped me just in time to save me an uncomfortable ducking on a dark winter's night in a cold November, which under the circumstances could not have been very enviable, setting aside the great probability of my ever being got out alive at all in such darkness – however, thank God, we arrived home in safety having felt our way pretty correctly- for we could not see it. I think, a darker night I never remember, we could not see our hands six inches from our eyes and coming out of a light house, having been in a light all the evening and scene of the above anecdote being overshadowed with immense walnut trees made the darkness still worse, so readers you may judge of the intensity of the darkness, in fact, it was almost "darkness that could be felt" and it was well nigh making me feel the consequences of it. Ever after this when keeping night school we carried a small hand lantern with us for safety. Our house was situated at the bottom of a hill a little more than half a mile in length and the road being straight, the whole length of it my mother could always see our light by looking out immediately on our arrival at the top of the hill some ten minutes before we arrive home. At Whitsuntide in this year (1846), having a week's holiday I and my father started off to Cambridge, and there being no conveyance whatever, we had to walk the 28 miles (from Shefford) on foot.

Downing Arms Inn (now a private residence)

We thought of going to the Downing Arms to sleep, which lay about midway between Shefford and Cambridge. We arrived there about 8o'clock in the evening, having had an early tea and started about four o'clock in the afternoon, but on our arrival at this place, we were surprised to find a grand set of merrymaking in regular rustic style – On enquiry we found it was the title feast day and every bed was let, they could not possibly oblige us with a bed. Here was music and dancing, singing and shouting, sports of all kinds and drink in abundance and the people belonging to the house as busy as bees, pleasure, mirth and joy appeared to light up the countenance of all present, who, apparently were enjoying themselves to their hearts' content.

> On the day we went to Cambridge
> At the Downing Arms, I trow
> The lads and lasses in their best
> Were dressed from top to toe
> They danced and sung the jocund song
> In garden and on green
> And nought but mirth and jollity
> Around us could be seen
> 'Twas thus they pass'd the pleasant time
> Nor thought of care and woe
> On the day we went to Cambridge
> Some few short years ago

Being thus disappointed of our lodging, we had no other alternative than to push forward to the next village which lay some distance on the road, so we took a little refreshment at the "scene of mirth" and left them to enjoy themselves, while we pursued our journey. We arrived ere long at a turnpike gate, we enquired at the house adjoining whether they could direct us to a lodging for the night, they could neither oblige us themselves, nor recommend us anywhere, but there happened to be a good-natured old dame in the house at the time, who stated that she was just going home (about half a mile further on our road) and that "out of compassion for the poor little boy who must be very tired", having walked about 15 miles since 4o'clock, "she would oblige us with a bed – thus your humble author and his father found a comfortable nights lodgings in the humble cot of the good natured old dame, for which we were very thankful – Early in the morning, we all arose and having partaken of a healthy dejeuner off the viandes with which the larder of the old lady supplied us, we, together with she and her son, who were going to market, started off again on our journey, having all the less to go, for our extended journey of the previous evening – we arrived at our destination before dinner, quite sound in wind and limb and none the worse for our walk.

Having spent our holiday as happily as we could at Cambridge and Cottenham we started off home again one afternoon –

reached the Downing Arms by dusk when we were fortunate enough to obtain a bed this time and found the place a little more quiet that when we were last there and early on the following day we left for Shefford, where we arrived safe and sound and found all at home quite well.

In the following years, my brother John James, was at home as his services being no longer required at St Anne's School – so, he having obtained another place as Assistant in St Pauls Schools at Cambridge – He and I started off for Cambridge, he to his situation and I for a fortnights holiday. It was on Easter Monday 1847, we had at that time obtained a house in the village of Meppershall not far from the School and close beside the churchyard, this made it much more comfortable for us with respect to our work. This fact will prepare the reader for the assertion that our journey was this time thirty one miles instead of twenty eight. We started at 7 a.m. and after a very hot journey succeeded in reaching Cambridge by 4 p.m. Having walked through the town we proceeded to the new Railway Station which had not been long opened. It was there that I first saw a "Railway Train" which I had heard so much talk of and it was there that the term "rails", "points", "sleepers" and other railway terms were practically illustrated to me, previous to which time I had not the most remote idea of what they could be. I also observed a number of posts along the line at equal distances with some ten or a dozen wires fastened to them and in the distance resembling a curved cobweb between two poles – On making enquiry I found that there were the Electric Telegraph wires. I was then lost in wonder as to how these wires could by any possible means be made to carry messages and signals for different purposes. I observed also that they were fastened to each pole so that they could not be moved and this puzzled me more. On asking <u>how</u> it was worked, everybody appeared to be as ignorant as myself:- they saw the wires and had been accustomed to seeing them for some time but were no more acquainted with its working than I was, who had never as much as seen the wires before. A series of conjectures and suppositions were advanced, but were as soon contradicted by a sight of the fixtures, at last they gave over: no one could enlighten my mind upon the matter and I was compelled to content myself in my ignorance, I expressed a very strong desire to be able to find out some day or other how the telegraph was worked.

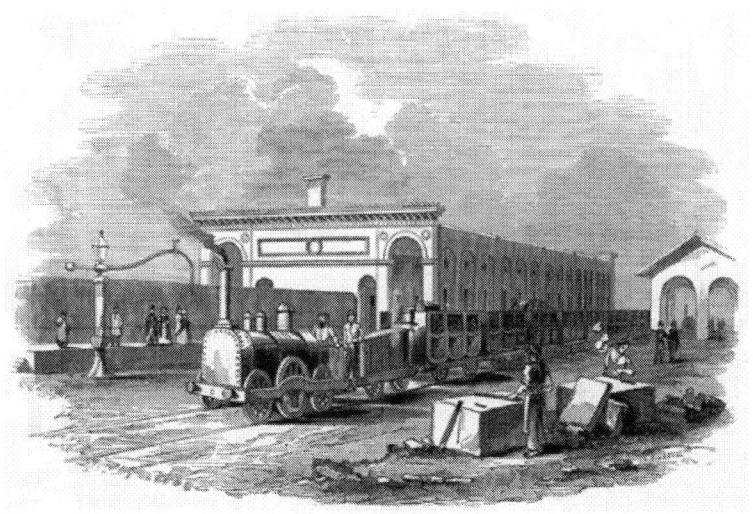

Cambridge railway station at about the time that the author would have seen it

The following morning my brother went with me nearly to the boundary of the Town on the road leading to Cottenham and there he left me – he to go back to his School, I to find my way as best I could to my father's relations. I had not left my brother more than a quarter of an hour before I came to a place where two roads met with the one I had just come formed the shape of a Y. I continued my course down the left hand road until I fancied, from what I recollected of my visit with my father the previous year, that I was on the wrong road, for I thought that I ought, by that time, to have arrived at Histon about 3 miles from Cambridge, so, on observing a gentleman on horseback I enquired of him whether I was on the right road from Cambridge to Cottenham – when to my great chagrin I found that I had taken the wrong road from the turnpike gate at the junction and that as there was a crossroad to lead into the other one I must return to the gate again. So, I retraced my steps as fast as I could and gained the junction – I then commenced again having lengthened by journey about 6 miles. I soon came to the long sought village of Histon and not long after entered Cottenham and having found my aunt's house I felt well inclined to assist them at a good dinner which was just smoking on the table. I enjoyed it much as also did I my holiday altogether, when however it soon rolled over and I must return to Meppershall, I walked to Cambridge one evening and slept there. Next day after dinner I left for home once more over the old well known road, every time that I had been this road previously I had had company with me but this time I was alone on foot with this long journey by me – however I knew my road well and was not afraid of losing my way so nothing daunted I stated about two or three o'clock. Having walked very leisurely I reached the old half way house the Downing Arms, about seven o'clock and it being very light, weather fine, roads good and not feeling at all fatigued I thought that I would venture to go a little further and chance getting a lodging, so having taken some refreshment, I made another start and reached the next village at dusk – I met some labourers at the commencement of the village and enquired of them whether I was likely to get a lodging for the night in the place, they expressed their doubts upon the subject, however they told me to enquire of a house they described as a short distance off in the village of Eyeworth such was the appelation of this lonely place, but the inhabitants pronounced it "Howarth". I went on but saw no house of the kind they had told me, so determined to ask at the very next house I came to. I did so and the answer was "Noa, we caent, but mayhap our folks next door may hev a bed ye moight mak use uv for the need, we'll goa an ax eef ye'll wait". I waited an the reply she brought me was – "Ees, ye can hev hafe a bed wi our naabur's son, eef ye loike". I expressed my gratitude for her kindness and proceeded to her "naabur's to find my "have a bed" in which I slept soundly for the night:- the father and son rose early in the morning and bade me "goodbye". I had breakfast with the old lady, who, en passant, was a motherly old dame and having settled my bill for accommodation, which I am certain did not pay for the breakfast I had eaten, I proceeded on my journey homewards, where I reached about noon = this was the last journey I made on that road, and at this time I was fourteen years of age or thereabouts.

I continued to assist my father in his school which prospered amazingly under our tuition – we made some very good scholars of the children - some of whom came 4 or 5 miles to school. We were respected by all the inhabitants both old and young, rich and poor. In the winter of 1847 we commenced evening school again – our old scholars rejoined us and were making still further progress, when we were compelled to leave Meppershall as my father had obtained a better situation at a place called Hoo near Rochester in the county of Kent, of which more, in the next chapter. Great sorrow and grief were expressed throughout the village at the idea of our leaving them after having been with them so long – they were one and all most sincerely attached to us, and the thought of our departure seemed to wound their very hearts- on the day we left, the minister – the Revd I.H. Howlett – (our previous one having removed to London) came to see us and remained all the time we were packing up altho' the house was full of things all higgledy piggledy; he could not bear the thought of parting with us - he seemed as if he could not leave us and he wandered about in and out of the house almost mute. Almost everyone shed tears at our departure – several children followed us a long way.

A few months before we left Meppershall I commenced the study of Algebra. I had a great desire to learn it and I resolved one day to ask Mr Howlett the Rector to give me a few lessons in it. I met him in the Shrubbery adjoining the house, as I was going from it and asked him "whether he would be so kind as to give me a few lessons in Algebra" – He looked at me with surprise and exclaimed "What ! James! – are you going to turn collegian?" – "As regards to that Sir," I replied "I cannot say, but nevertheless I should like to understand Algebra" – "Very well James, if you come to me tomorrow I shall be very glad to give you a few lessons". I thanked him and on the morrow I accordingly went to receive my first lesson in Algebra – in which study I continued to persevere under his tuition up to the time we left the place by which time I had progressed as far as "Simple Equations". On our leaving he presented me with "Hall's Algebra" which is published at 7/6* and to my father he

---

* 7/6 or 7s 6d is 37.5p in decimal currency. [Eds]

presented a "Book of commentaries on the gospels" as tokens of his esteem for us.

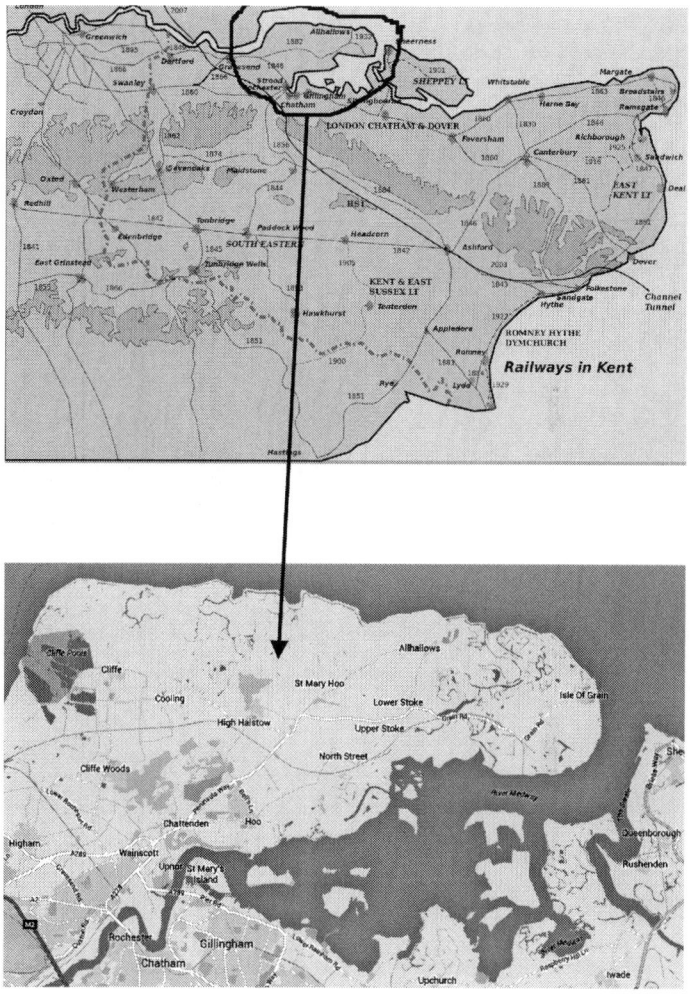

Upper map: Kent with the Hoo Peninsula circled. London is just off the top left

Lower map: Hoo Peninsula and Medway. The towns of Rochester, Chatham and Gillingham can be seen at the bottom of the picture.

Chapter 5th

We started from Meppershall on the 30th day of December 1847 and arrived in London the same evening, put up there for the night and the following morning we started off again, the roads being rather worse than those of the previous day and the County of Kent so much more hilly − we could not get further than Gravesend that night − here we slept in the waggon and had to deal with the most hard hearted, uncivil, abrupt, independent and disobliging people we ever met with = not a bit nor drop of anything could be got, but at an enormous and extortionate price = not even a drop of warm water could be obtained to make a cup of tea or coffee or anything else without paying for it and that very dearly = if we wanted tea or coffee we must buy it ready made or go without = and it was with difficulty that we begged sufficient hot water to make a little sop for the baby then 3 months old or a little less:- at daybreak we started on our way for Hoo where we arrived soon after noon = and in order to reach our appointed residence with the waggon it was imperative that we drive it round by a very narrow lane, the wheels of the waggon sinking into the mud up to their centres, there were some carts bringing stones to throw down in it to make it more solid − we had not proceeded far before our waggon got stuck fast in the mud. In trying to pull it out one of the two horses broke the chain connecting the collar with the shaft. We asked the men at work with their carts, in each of which were 2 or 3 horses and not a quarter the load we had, whether they would give us a little assistance − they said that they dared not for their masters would not let them if they knew it − however, one of them at last ventured to help us out and we succeeded in getting round to the house situate close beside the Medway, into which at high water, one might throw a stone from the house: we entered our new abode on the New Year's day of 1848 = it not situate a quarter of a mile from the school.

The village of Hoo lies on the northern bank of the River Medway about 12 miles westward from Sheerness and 3 miles eastward from Rochester = About midway between Rochester and Hoo stands Upnor Castle a very old building, where a few soldiers are at present stationed − it takes its name from the neighbouring village of Upnor = There is a powder magazine attached to the castle which faces the river and at the back there is an extensive garden - passing on still nearer to Hoo along the coast we find the remains of an old fort, now entirely in ruins = It happens to have been built with red bricks the walls being of an immense thickness, judging from the appearance of the masses of brickwork found about the place = all the building has disappeared and here and there may be seen an immense block of brickwork buried in the ground, having apparently formed the foundation of the building. The ground here being about 30 – 40 feet above the level of high water marks and supported and preserved from the water by a perpendicular wall of extraordinary thickness also of redbrick, it is natural to suppose that the building must have been very elevated and commanded a good range down the river:- the wall bears numerous marks of cannon balls having been thrown at it and towards the bottom of it where the water washes it at high tide, it is worn away and completely washed out for full three feet backwards. At the eastern end of the wall was a kind of hut also of brick with an arched roof and which afforded a good shelter for persons who were walking that way from a shower of rain or from the wind from any quarter except the south, the roof of it has now practically fell (*sic*) in and blocked up the entrance. On the other side of the Medway and immediately opposite this old ruin there is the fort of Gillingham in good presentation. Soldiers are stationed here, who, when the river is clear of vessels often practice firing their cannon at the old wall across the water. The top of this old wall commands a most extensive view as also a most splendid one. Immediately on the right (facing the water and looking southward) lies the village of Upnor and behind it the village and church of Frindsburyon a hill, behind this rise the spires of some of the churches of Rochester. A view may likewise be had of the Cathedral and the old Castle Tower of Rochester. Following with the eye, the scenery a little more to the southward we have a fine view of the town and the Dockyards of Chatham and the town of Brompton on the hill. In the river of which pursues a very crooked course from the Dockyard towards Sheerness lie a number of large men of war waiting to be called in their turns into active service in case of an emergency most of them being new = next in view on the hill opposite us, comes the large open space adjoining the Chatham barracks and Dockyards known by the name of "Chatham Lines" – here it is that the reviews take place and a very good view of them may be had from the Old Fort Wall, especially if the wind be favourable to carry away the smoke, with the assistance of a telescope the movements of the troops could be narrowly watched = near the "Lines" may be seen rising the spire of the new church of Brompton built a few years since. Then comes the Gillingham Fort above named = the village of Gillingham almost buried in trees the Church Tower just raising itself into view, and then turning to the extreme left, if it be a clear day, the shipping may be plainly seen at Sheerness at a distance of about 13 miles, and the village of Hoo about 1 mile from the observer. It is stated by some of the inhabitants that in the time of an invasion of England by a fleet, said to have belonged to the Danes or Dutch – there was a very strong chain stretched across the Medway from the Gillingham Fort to the Old Fort which is now in ruins and that upon the fleet's arrival there they were stopped in their course and annihilated by the two forts – they having completely destroyed the fleet.

Taking of the *Royal Charles* by the Dutch fleet under Admiral Michiel de Ruiter (painting by Jan van Leyden)

I have never been able to trace the truth of this tradition – nor in whose reign it occurred neither under whose command the fleet was, nor under what circumstances the invasion took place, therefore I cannot vouch for the truth of the local tradition*. The village of Hoo was anciently called Hoo St Werburgh. It has a very ancient church with a square tower upon which rises a spire made of wood cut into wedges all of which are neatly filled and nailed together = This spire has been struck twice or thrice by lightning and set on fire – it has now a lightning conductor = inside the church may be seen some very ancient monumental brasses, with figures of different persons cut in them and inscriptions in old English upon them = there are some very quaint carved heads in the woodwork near the roof which look very conspicuous. In the chancel and also in the body of the church are two openings in the wall at some 12 feet from the ground, where, it is said, penance was performed in ancient times = there is also a gallery of modern construction, a neat little organ, which it was the duty of my father or myself to play on Sundays during our residence there = In a very large book on the topography of Kent in the British Museum, may be found the following curious lines which give my readers a rough idea of the ancient state of the place some hundreds of years ago –

"Whoever pays a visite to How
Besides pilfering sailors will fynde dirt enow"

There are not many sailors at the place now, as the principal seafaring place is Chatham, but at the time the above lines were written, perhaps Chatham was not in the flourishing state it has now arrived at and very likely the village of "How" might have been established by sailors and fishermen = it is very singular, but all the footways about here appear to be made almost exclusively of cockle-shells and the whole land about here seems to be full of them. There is one walk leading from the Church down to the waterside called by the inhabitants "The Cockleshell" made entirely of these shells = so from this it may be inferred that at one time a large fishing trade might have been carried on here, and the shells of the cockles made into roads and footpaths being peculiarly adopted for the purpose thus giving rise to the expression "pilfering sailors" – When the tide is down

---

* During the Anglo-Dutch war Admiral Michiel de Ruiter, led a fleet which attacked the Medway towns during the period 10 – 20 June 1667. He broke the chains and made his way as far as Upnor Castle, destroying several ships and taking the *Royal Charles* as a prize. [Eds]

there is left plainly visible for about a mile from the shore the mud over which the tide rises and covers it – this might have given rise to part of the sentence, namely that the visitor would find "dirt enow" for truly when the tide has ebbed there is plenty of mud to be seen = Thus the old couplet is very likely exemplified by the present appearance and state of things.

The School consisted of two rooms, one over the other, the ground floor for the boys and elder girls (mixed) in the morning and the upper room for the younger ones of both sexes. In the afternoon all the boys occupied the lower and all the girls the upper room. Attached to the school was a fine playground enclosed by a brick wall – the upper room was entered from the playground, without going into the lower room, by means of a flight of stairs at the end of the building. Here we had a much larger number of scholars than at Meppershall but a very rough collection – they were the most surly, ill behaved, disobedient set of children we had ever met with – At prayer times in the afternoon (which we said just before leaving school) scarcely was the last word commenced before they were all up, jumping over the forms and running after their caps, throwing them in all directions, in fact the place was complete "bedlam". We saw very evidently that we had our work to do to tame them and break them in – After some difficulty we succeeded in making a little alteration in their conduct and taught them a little manners, which before were quite out of the question, and in the course of one year we had effected, by God's blessing on our labours, such an entire change that the school was not like the same in any respect whatever = I continued to study in my leisure time and persevered in my Algebra and several other branches of education and I and my father managed to help each other very well indeed and we set ourselves to mutual instruction, what one could not find out the other did and thus we endeavoured to improve ourselves that we might be the more able to impart that knowledge to our scholars and as we had no one to teach us we were compelled to satisfy ourselves with such books as we happened to have in our possession. These were our teachers.

The place being so near the water and being very damp and

marshy the inhabitants suffered very much from the Ague* and it was no uncommon occurrence for 2 or 3 children to be compelled to be sent home from school, having had an attack come on them in the school. We had not been there many months before it commenced in our family upon my younger brother William, it reduced him terribly and he never thoroughly recovered from it, but after a few more months it brought on fever and fits, he was laid up for some time with it, but began to recover a little, so that he came down stairs again, but poor little fellow, his was completely distorted and twice its natural size – in fact we could scarcely have recognised him had we not known who he was; this slight recovery was but a final struggle – He was taken in another fit of screaming convulsions and at last, by the great providence of the Almighty he was released from his pains, and I have every reason to believe was received into those realms where reign neither trials or sickness and where all is peace and joy and love. This was a happy release for him. The last sound by way of speech that I heard from his lips was that he was in his agony whispering the 'Lords Prayer' but which he had not power to articulate distinctly. Poor dear little fellow, his screams were dreadful – they were heard some hundred yards distant and as long as I have my reasoning faculties preserved me, I shall <u>never</u> forget his death bed scene. The interesting little fellow was thus released from his agony on the 4th day of January in the year 1849 and was buried in the Churchyard of Hoo, where his remains now lie immediately behind the vestry. Although we had cause to grieve at parting with him at so interesting an age of 7 years and 1 month, yet still we also had cause to rejoice to thing that the Almighty had in his providential arrangements received him to himself and raised him from this world of care, sickness and sorrow to meet his Saviour in the air and to enjoy in those blissful realms the joys and blessings of which "eye hath not seen, nor ear heard, neither hath it entered into the hear of man even to conceive". In a very little time after my brother's first attack it fell to my lot to be attacked with ague and I continued to have it at intervals for nearly a year and half, during which time my health was much affected. It was very evident the climate

---

* Swamp fever or malaria is due to the anopheles atroparvus mosquito. It thrives in saline marshes and was endemic in this area [Eds]

and the air did not agree with me, so I endeavoured to get a situation to which end I answered several advertisements – but to no purpose – towards the latter part of the year 1848 I saw that an assistant clerk in a mercantile house in the City of London was required and I did think I should have obtained it but I was disappointed again. I continued to study in the hope of hearing of something sometime or another to my advantage. The son of the Clergyman's wife (by a previous husband) named Robert Avelyn, gave me a little more insight into Algebra and I progressed under his tuition through Simple Equations and commenced Quadratic Equations. Altho' I had always been brought up under the instruction of Christian and religious parents, and had been taught religious principles in the Schools I had attended at Cambridge, and altho' I had no associates but those of strict moral integrity and was never allowed by my parents to be out with any others but of this description – still for all this it was not till the beginning of the year 1849 that I was brought to a true sense of "the exceeding sinfulness of sin" and was led to see in a clean light my need for a Saviour, and to feel that I had been hitherto living in ignorance of my real position in the sight of Him to whom "all hearts are open, all desires known and from whom no secrets are hid" = This change was effected by the Holy Spirit though the instrumentality of a sermon preached by the minister of our Parish the Rev[d] I. D'Urban from the 8th verse of the 16th chapter of the gospel according to St. John:- the words were as follows:- And when he (the comforter) is come, he shall convince (or reprove) the world of sin; of righteousness, and of judgement". It was from this text that the sermon was made which was so firmly impressed upon my mind that I have never forgotten it, and it was the means, as I have stated above, of "<u>convincing me of sin</u>" and leading me more earnestly to see for a Saviour in Jesus Christ, by and through whom alone we can be saved = In March of this year (1849) is was intended by the Bishop or Rochester to hold a Confirmation for the District in which Hoo was included – accordingly, having arrived in my 16th year I was admitted at the end of February as a candidate for Confirmation. There was about 16 altogether male and female. We met every Sunday before service to receive instruction from the minister and to be examined in the things particularly necessary to so important a ceremony. The day of confirmation having arrived, namely the 27th of March 1849, we all proceeded in order to the neighbouring village of High Halstow, where the Confirmation was to take place, - This place stands on a very high hill about 3 miles north of Hoo and commands a view of the Thames and Cooling Castle on its banks – on the north:- of Hoo, and the Medway, on the south:- and of the Nore and Sheerness on the east:- very pleasantly situated indeed and very healthy – The church which is not very large, is very ancient and it was in this ancient edifice that I was confirmed, thereby releasing my sponsors (one of whom, my godfather, en passant, had hanged himself) from their charges and taking upon myself the responsibility of the promises they had made for me, when I was unable to make them myself, but, which having attained a sufficient age to do so, I had now come to renew in my own person. It is rather a singular coincidence, that the young woman with whom I afterwards became more intimately acquainted, with whom I corresponded incessantly for several years, and to whom (as will be seen hereafter in this work) I was married, was also confirmed in the same church, on the same day, and at the same hour as myself! = I continued to assist my father in his school at Hoo until the New Year of 1850, when in a day or two my father accompanied me to London to receive final answer in reference to the assistant mastership of the St Pancras National School, London for which situation I had applied in answer to an advertisement. After having been before the Committee there assembled and answered several questions – they decided in my favour and my engagement was to commence forthwith. I returned to Hoo with my father to obtain my clothes etc and on 7th of January I prepared to start to pursue my new employment away from home, it being the first situation I had ever been in away from home. I will now with your permission take leave of my parents and friends and family connections and leave them to continue their avocations in the state of life which they are placed by the providence of God, and endeavour to relate to you the course, I afterwards pursued when I had no longer my parents' eyes to watch over me. So now my dear readers, you will join with me in bidding a farewell to my parents and the rest of the family.

Chapter 6th

St Pancras National School is situate in Southampton Street, Euston Square about equidistant between St Pancras Church and the terminus of the London and North Western Railway and not more than three minutes walk from either of the abovementioned places. The School itself is a long building occupying with the grounds about half the extend of the left hand side of the street, entering from the Seymour Street end. The Boys School is the first approached – adjoining to this is the Master's House, then contiguous to this is the Mistresses' House – the two houses projecting farther than the schoolrooms forming the centrepiece of the building the doorways being under a portico. Next to the mistresses' House comes the Girls room = Behind the Master's and Mistresses' Houses were built in 1851 and 2 classrooms, one for each school and entered by a door from each room, and there being a door in the partition between the classrooms, there was a communication thus made between the Boys' and Girls' Rooms behind the houses without going outside into the open air. Behind the Girls's Schoolroom an infant school was erected in 1852: a very neat, convenient little building. At the head of the Boys' Schoolroom, the space corresponding with the site of the Infant School on the other side was occupied by a long shed about 6 (*yds ???*) wide with a seat (*???*) the entire length of the school for the children in case of the weather, the remaining portion was paved with wood pavement furnished with poles at either end for gymnastic exercises for the boys. In the interior of the Boys' room there was a cupboard containing a library of one hundred and fifty volumes, for the use of the children of both schools by the payment of one halfpenny and of which I was constituted librarian = the room was also furnished with parallel desks – blackboards and easels. A set of Hullah's music sheets and other school requisites = it has two patent stoves one at each end of the room = it is lighted by gas, conducted from the street thro' a meter, and traversing the beams drops in four pendant pipes, each of four burners = The master's desk is a very large one – it consists of a large platform mounted by three steps on either side, upon which is place a moveable desk. In the event of a public meeting being held in the room (which is of frequent occurrence) this moveable desk is taken down and substituted by a smaller flat square table and covered with a green baize – the platform is placed in a suitable position and is capable of accommodating about twenty persons each seated on a chair. On such occasions as these, the boarding round it is covered with red stuff (like that in general use in churches for curtains etc) with a wide fringe – all the forms (which are screwed to the ground) are taken up and placed in a semicircular manner around the platform. This with the gas all lighted up – the room crowded with people and a spirited speech – all tends to present to the eye and ear a very imposing spectacle. During the time that the Church was under repair the service was performed in this room which would accommodate nearly a thousand persons. We had on the School Books about 300 children's names about 250 of whom were generally present = It was conducted by first and second master and an assistant. The salary of the first master was £100 per annum, that of the second £50 and that of the assistant (which situation I filled) £25 = I commenced on January 7th 1850 the duties devolving upon me which were to give a general superintendence over the School, to assist in keeping good order and to see that the teachers kept their classes at work, and to give lessons to any class I chose upon different subjects, occasionally giving as object lesson to the juniors in the class room, and oftentimes a music lesson to the seniors upon Hullah's* system of teaching singing = one of the singing classes having been delivered to my charge. What a contrast did these duties present to those of my former position in my father's school, where there were so few scholars, so little to do and such a poor variety of subjects which we were compelled to suit to the tastes and circumstances of the country children! Such a contrast was very pleasing to me, as it gave me much greater scope for my abilities and enabled me to put into practice the things I had been studying at home, which I had

---

*John Pyke Hullah, born Worcester in 1812 and died in London 1884 became a champion of the Wilhem's fixed-doh method of teaching sight-singing and held classes in and near London to teach it with enormous initial success, the system being one of those that are attractively easy for the beginner and reveal their difficulties only later. He became the Government inspector of music in teacher training colleges, but his system was eventually replaced by Curwen's more psychologically true tonic sol-fa. (from P.A. Scholes "Oxford Companion to Music") [Eds]

hitherto been unable to do. I had a collection of bright, sharp lads under me now who would be pleased with any new subject I liked to introduce and thus it gave me encouragement to continue my studies still further and at the same time rooted still more in my mind those I had already learned and not this only, but being the first time I had ever been from home, and therefore, entering as I was upon the world upon my own responsibility, I felt it my duty and intention to do my utmost to win the esteem of my employers and the affections of the scholars under me, as, having now made a start in the world, I felt that it would be equal to robbery to return to my parents roof again for support, These feelings acted as spurs to my conduct and by the blessing of God I was enabled to accomplish my objects in every respect. I devoted all my leisure time to hard study. Unfortunately on the twentieth day of February 1859 I met with an accident by which I was kept from my duties for nearly 6 weeks much to my sorrow and chagrin, as I began to get so comfortable in my situation and to be respected by those with whom I had any intercourse in the prosecution of my duties. I had up to this time lived with my Aunt (my mother's sister Mary Howlett) in White Lion Building Islington. I will just give a few facts relative to my accident = It must be understood that under the Schoolroom there is a cellar to keep the firing in − to which entrance is gained by a double folding trap-door in the floor = thence down a flight of stone steps. I was standing about a foot from the edge of this when one of the boys went down the cellar and left the door open − this without my knowledge − Upon finishing my conversation with the Master I stepped backwards in order to go to the other end of the room and was immediately precipitated to the bottom of the cellar and in my fall struck my left knee against the opposite half of the flap (which was closed) and cut it to the muscle just below the knee-cap, the wound was about an inch and a quarter in length and I could lay the first joint of my little finger on the muscle − The master on seeing the wound ordered me to the surgeons at the corner of Euston Square (Mr Meyrryweather). He referred me to the University College Hospital. On coming out of his shop I was met at the door by the Head Master of the School (Mr Lettice) who accompanied me to the Hospital (to which I walked). The surgeon examined the wound, found no bones broken, or anything else seriously injured. He strapped it up and ordered me to keep my leg straight and not to walk about until it was healed. I returned to the school with Mr Lettice who instructed the second master (Mr Wiswould) to accompany me home to Islington. Here I remained for a fortnight, when, the wound having sufficiently healed, I started off by rail to Strood, for Hoo, to remain at home until I was enabled to resume my duties again. Here I remained nearly month, kept myself quiet and bathed my knee 2 or 3 times a day with cold spring water. At the expiration of this time I was sufficiently strong on my legs to return – which I did and was heartily welcomed by all my acquaintances. On my return I went to reside at No 74 Charlton Street New Road, St. Pancras. During my first residence in London I had been exceedingly cautious in going about, having great fear of loosing myself, however, by degrees I found myself gain confidence and after a short time I could find my way about all the principal thoroughfares in London with tolerable ease and correctness.

I should have said before that on the 24th December 1849 just before I left home I received a very kind note from Miss Ann Charlotte Smith, a frequent visitor to our house (of very respected and honest parentage and who were placed in very tolerable circumstances) in which she appeared to express a great interest on my behalf and sincerely hoped that I should be successful in the situation I was seeking at St Pancras. The circumstance passed and nothing further was thought of the letter by me.

After being in London a few months I began to look out for some intelligent acquaintances with whom I could associate myself and thus pass in a pleasing and profitable manner my leisure hours of an evening. I formed acquaintance with a Mr Edward Thomas Morgan, assistant master at the East St Pancras School and a Mr Thomas Castleman, Assistant master of Agar Town National School. In these two persons I found both intelligent and agreeable companions and (as) the obtaining of a "Government Certificate" was the current topic amongst Schoolmasters, we determined each to try our fortune at studying for one. Accordingly we Established amongst ourselves a "Mutual

Improvement Society" and we met every evening at the house of Mr Castleman for the purpose of study for about 2 1/2 or 3 hours – We drew up "Rules and Regulations" and a "Time Table" setting forth the subject for each evening's study (Sundays excepted) and the time allotted to each subject = thus we pursued a regular course and the consequence was rapid progress by all parties. After a time we (at their request) admitted Messrs Deacock, Robinson and Bulliman, but we were sorry for it afterwards = The first of these parties was a Cabinet and Pianoforte maker, the second a carpenter and the last an artist. We continued very cordially together for a short time pursuing our regular course of study until one of them introduced a female acquaintance one evening = this became of more frequent occurrence until in a short time a friend of hers was brought and the topic of study and conversation being directed into another course far different from that set down in our "Time Table" I resolved to break up, if possible, our Society altogether. I determined upon a scheme which succeeded admirably. I mentioned my intentions to no one, not even to Mr Morgan, my most sincere friend. I wrote a letter (in a disguised handwriting which they could not detect) as coming from one of the Clergymen of the District and addressed to all the members of the Society, but more pointedly to those of the members who were engaged in tuition, pointing out the disgrace they brought upon their profession, and showing that in it they most assuredly put on only "a form of godliness" and when away from the scenes of their employment they were every evening acting in direct violation of all "godly" principles – assuring them that the writer of the letter had watched their proceedings very narrowly and that unless an immediate change was wrought in their conduct, he would present himself amongst them some evening in person and call them to account for their conduct and concluded by signing it "A Lover of Sobriety". This was received by Mr Castleman and on the evening of its receipt (by post) after the usual minutes of the previous evening had been read all the members present and they seated comfortably, Mr Castleman intimated that he had received a letter by that day's post bearing reference to our Society and that he deemed it his duty to read its contents aloud that all might hear it and decide what was to be done. He read it and all eyes were at first intently fixed upon him and then wandered about the room, each in his turn fixed upon one of his brother numbers, and again upon Mr C. - He having finished, a discussion arose as to the author of it = they reviewed the position of each of the Ministers in the parish with reference to his capability and opportunity of watching our proceedings and in the end came to no conclusion which proved anything satisfactory. Some advocated that we reform our proceedings and continue the society. I, Morgan and Castleman advocated that we discontinue it altogether, and again the opposition were for keeping it on, and by that means finding out by his "personal attendance" who the author of the letter was. We three persisted in our determination to break it up altogether, as the letter pointed especially to us and we were compelled by our duty to God and the nature of our calling to keep ourselves aloof from all such like proceedings. We, therefore, being three for, and three against it, discussed the matter for some time, when I proposed that, as we were the originators of the Society, the oldest members, and as the opposition were only by our consent admitted into the society, it was our right and privilege to come to a decision seeing that the two sides were equal in numbers – therefore in consideration of the foregoing claims it was our intention to discontinue the Meetings from that very night and accordingly the Society was broken up. This was the happy issue under God's guidance of the scheme adopted by me for that purpose. It is not known even, to this day, by any one of them who was the author of that eventful letter. After this time I and my friend Morgan studied with each other in his house with increased ardour and made extremely satisfactory progress in numerous branches of science, mathematics and history together with the usual subjects taught in National Schools and required of Schoolmasters in order to pass an examination for a "Government Certificate. We were occasionally joined by Mr Castleman. About this time I obtained a quantity of copying to do for a lawyer for a few weeks the proceeds of which were very useful in purchasing some books that I required = it was in the purchase of these that nearly all my spare money (which was very little) was employed.   One of our Curates The Rev[d]. F.I. Staniforth gave me a large Bound Book of Italian Operas to Copy. This occupied me a whole winter in my leisure hours. It filled nearly 250 pages of large sized manuscript music paper (16 staves deep). For this, when completed, I received the sum of nearly four pounds with which I furnished myself with a suit of black cloth, for as my salary was but £25 per year or about 9/7* per week I had little spare money for clothes – however with a half sovereign from home occasionally I managed very comfortably, as I lived with a very good motherly old lady, who knew how to make the best of everything and how to economise and with Dr Cotton I can now say.

> " Our portion was not large indeed
> But then how little did I need
> For Nature's calls were few
> In this the art of living lies
> To want no more than will suffice
> And make that little do "

It was upon this principle that I continued to live very comfortably upon my small salary during period of two year and a half, being the time that I continued at this school.

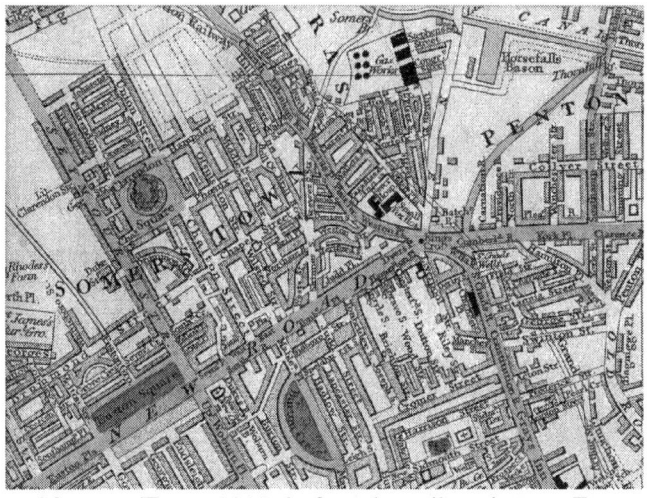

Map of Somers Town 1837, before the rail stations at Euston, St Pancras and Kings Cross obliterated many of the streets shown here. St Pancras (new) Church and Southampton Street are just off the bottom left corner.

---

* 9 shillings and 7 old pence is just less than £0.48 [Ed]

The Polygon, Somers Town 1850 (engraving by Joseph Swain
A scene that the author might have recognised

A view of the entrance to Euston Square Station

Chapter 7th

By the influence and kind intercession of the Revd Lawford W.T. Dale Curate of Saint Pancras, and who had the management of the Schools entrusted to him by the Vicar (the Revd Canon Dale) his father – he having too many other things to engage his attention, which prevented him from attending to the Schools, I obtained a Ticket of Admission to the reading Room of the British Museum.

Canon Dale from Illustrated London News 1859

This was to me a very valuable acquisition, as I could there obtain any Book I required to read or take notes and extracts from. I used to attend the Reading Room every Saturday – accompanied by my friend Mr Morgan who had also obtained a ticket of admission. The greatest difficulty I experienced was the finding in the Catalogue any book I might require, which is so complicated that unless some one had given me an insight into its arrangement, I think I should never have understood it. Even after having been initiated into the Old and New Catalogues I found great difficulty from the works being placed so out of the general alphabetical order, more especially in the Old Catalogue, however, I managed pretty well and could generally find the most important books I required, being supplied with conveniences for writing in the shape of tables, chairs, ink etc and being generally accompanied by my portfolio of plain paper I made several "notes" which I found at different times to be very useful to me. During the time I visited this Reading Room and having within my reach works of every description my dear Brother (John James*) and I kept up an "Educational Correspondence". We in turn proposed a set of questions to each other, and in turns answered them to the best of our ability, I having the greatest privilege of acquiring information. If any difficult subject was proposed or if anything met us with which we wre not acquainted, I made research in the Reading Room and in the Catalogue for works upon that subject, and having obtained them in the usual manner (by a check ticket with all particulars copied from the Catalogue) endeavoured to solve the mysterious subject and generally succeeded in doing so. Thus for some months we continued this mode of self improvements by posts.

While I was still in the habit of attending the British Museum I joined a Discussion Society at the Saint Johns Wood, consisting of some 7 or 8 members, the majority of whom were schoolmasters or assistants. The subjects chosen for the essays, which the members wrote in turns, being chiefly historical ones. It led me like the rest to search into History for arguments and facts upon which to found my opinions and thereby argue either for or against the Essayist. The Office of Secretary was entrusted by unanimous vote to Mr F. Timbrell. The amount paid by each member was sixpence per month, for the purpose of supplying the requisite ink, paper, firing and the room = A financial report was made every three months by the Secretary and Treasurer. The first Essay that I produced, or ever attempted to write, was upon the question whether or not the discovery of American has

---

* John James Graves eventually became the first President of the National Union of Elementary Teachers, now known as the National Union of Teachers [Eds]

proved beneficial to this country = Upon this occasion there were 7 members present. 3 opposed me, two supported me and the Chairman, not being allowed to discuss, but only to be appealed to in case of equal contest to give his casting vote. He, being not a very good scholar and one who took little interest in the discussion which had for a long time been so hotly contested by equal forces, gave his vote on the side of the opposition. Thus causing me to lose the decision in my favour. However, I still continued by same opinion, as did also my supporters, on the subject viz. That the discovery of America had proved of decided benefit to this country. My next essay was upon the "Character of Charlemagne" = whether he, taking all his actions as one whole, deserved commendation = This point I gained, and it was decided that he did deserve our praise and commendation = My third essay was upon the "Character of Charles II of England" whether or not he was at heart a Roman Catholic, in spite of his outward professions to Protestantism. This was never read, nor discussed as the summer was advancing, and the Society dissolved before my turn came again to read it. With the balance of our Funds and by each member adding a trifling sum to it, we were enabled to hold a grand supper at Christmas 1851 in the Strand. We were each allowed to take a friend on his paying the sum of two shillings and sixpence. We had a most splendid and delicious repast of the good things of this world, served up in the best possible manner and to which twelve of us sat down, and I did justice. After dinner (or rather supper at 8.0pm) was finished we had our desert and plenty of wine – and after having drunk the usual toasts of health to the Queen, Prince Albert, the Army and Navy – the Society and Officials personally – and the hour of midnight having arrived, we received notice of the same from the host, and separated, each very well satisfied with the proceedings of the evening.

The general system then raging of placing schools under "Government Inspection" found its way into Saint Pancras, and it was resolved to place our School under Government. The consequence was that ours being such a very large school it was entitled to receive 5 pupil Teachers, or apprentices and therefore, having those, the services of a 3rd master was no longer required.

Accordingly on Lady Day* 1852 I received notice from the Committee that my services would not be required after midsummer day next ensuing. I advertised in the "National Society Monthly Paper" for a situation as Assistant Master of a Large School or master of a small school in the country. I received several answers to my advertisements. In one case I had to go to Mr Wilson, the Head Master of the Westminster Training Institution to be examined. After having satisfactorily answered all questions put to me by him I went home, leaving him to communicate his opinion to his friends. I received a letter from the Gentleman stating that his friend Mr Wilson thought that I was "too young for the appointment" but that "my abilities were very good". In two other cases I was deemed too young for the situations = and in a fourth I held out to myself most sanguine hopes of success = This was a school at a place called Cleobury Mortimer in Shropshire = I received an answer to my advertisement from the Clergyman of that place (whose school would be vacant for a master at Midsummer) requesting me to forward testimonials of character, ability etc which I did. A letter from him informed me that they were very satisfactory and that I was one of 12 chosen for further consideration. A few days elapsed and I received intelligence that I was one of 6, this was a little more encouragement for me and still holding out hopes I would not seek anything else = About a week after, which was passed in the utmost anxiety and suspense – I received another letter stating that they required "specimens of linear drawing" and adding that I had but one opponent. I sent the required specimens, and anxiously did I await a final decision of the matter one way or another = The following week the "long looked for" arrived – when, I read – "I have great regret in informing you that the Committee have decided upon your opponent to fill the office of master of their school, on account of his having the advantage over yourself of one year in age, and at the same time, am instructed to inform you that the Committee are highly pleased with your testimonials and abilities and trust that you will soon succeed in obtaining employment. I herein enclose your testimonials" – etc - . My feeling can be more easily imagined than described, to think that after five weeks

---

* 25th March [Eds]

suspense and uncertainty I should meet with another disappointment, but so it was everything appeared to go against me and had I not put my trust in the Almighty Disposer of Events I might have sunk under my load of grief and disappointment.

During my stay in the school at St Pancras I had become enamoured of a young woman named "Sarah Malham" living in service at Saint John's Wood. I continued my addresses to her for some months until she left London and went to live in Berkshire = we continued our correspondence for a few weeks on usual terms, but all of a sudden she discontinued writing to me. I wrote her two or three letters, but for some cause or other unknown to me, or from no cause at all, she did not condescend to answer my letters, therefore, however painful to me at the time (for I was very fond of her) I was compelled to give up all hopes of ever seeing, or hearing from her again, thus our correspondence was abruptly broken off, and from that day to this I have never heard of her whereabouts nor whether she is dead or alive, or what became of her.

Time is ever swift on the wing and in its natural course my time grew short and at last Midsummer Day arrived and with it the end of my Schoolmaster's duties. But worse than all was, I had not been able up to that time to obtain a situation = and when I left the school I knew not what to do = The thought of going home to my parents, of being again dependent upon them for subsistence, when at an age at which I ought to be earning my own livelihood and the dark prospect before me, all tended to weigh down my spirits, and cause me much anxiety and uneasiness, and for which I appeared to have no remedy. What was I to do? <u>Must</u> I go home? Was there <u>no</u> alternative? Was there <u>no</u> means of my obtaining employment? These and many other questions of similar import came rushing to my mind and left me as they found me, I being unable to answer them satisfactorily. Having now left the school and having time on my hands all day, I resolved upon writing some specimens of my handwriting, ornamental and plain – and with these search the City and see if I could not obtain a Clerkship in either a merchant's or a lawyer's or law stationer's office. I accordingly started off one morning, determined not to return home, if possible, till I had obtained a situation of some kind or other – anything rather than be a burden on my parents. I enquired at numerous offices, but no one knew of any person requiring a clerk. I had enquired at nearly twenty different places all to no purpose when I went to a Law Stationers at the corner of Bell Yard in Carey Street, by the name of "Heraud" = To him I stated my case and he after a little conversation said he might want a clerk in the course of a few weeks, but he did not just then require one = however in consideration of my position and circumstances he would agree to take me then and there for a salary of 12/= per week*. This I readily accepted, it being nearly half a crown per week more than my previous salary:- and the agreement being made I went to work at 9 o'clock the following morning, but what a change! In my school I had only to work from 9 a.m. till 12 and from two till 4 pm in winter and 5pm in summer = but here I had to work from 9am till 9pm with one hour for dinner when not busy and none when busy, sometimes I was writing the whole of the time and again, sometimes I had very little to do, but had to be there in case of any work coming in. It would often happen that, in the evening just before I was about to leave, a great quantity of work would come in and must be done immediately = then I had to turn to and work overtime for which I was paid according to the quantity and description of the work done at a certain stated sum per folio. Thus I generally earned a few shillings every week, but it was very hard work for me after having been used to the School duties for so long, in fact, I might say, all my lifetime. However, I managed to do very well, and to give satisfaction to my Employer**. It happened that during my employment here, one of the pupil Teachers of the Saint Pancras School informed me that a friend of his had told him that there were some vacancies in "the Electric Telegraph Company" at Lothbury, London for Clerks = I was persuaded by him to apply for one of the vacancies and thinking that personal application is at all times better than letter, I resolved to apply personally at the office at the earliest opportunity, for

---

* Twelve shillings or 60p in decimal currency [Eds]

** It was at about this time that Graves compiled a short autobiography, probably as a personal statement for employment [Eds]

which I eagerly watched. Having to take home some work done to a solicitor in Falcon Street, City I thought this a good opportunity for applying, as I had nothing to do at my office having just finished up all. I accordingly went and after staying some time was introduced to the Superintendent = I was instructed to fill up a "Form of Application" and to obtain testimonials = which I did = and after having written an exercise from dictation - from the leading article of the Sun newspaper – I was informed that there were not at present any vacancies but undoubtedly there would be shortly and that they would send for me. I then left referring them to three or four parties as references as to character. In the course of two or three weeks I received a letter informing me that I could then enter upon my duties as "learner" and when competent I should be appointed but until I had passed my examination I should receive no salary. I received this letter at the beginning of the second week before Christmas 1852 and accordingly informed my Employer that I should require to leave his employ, if convenient on Saturday night following = stated my reasons and he said, it was the duty of everyone to look after themselves and that, therefore he could not blame me for endeavouring to better my circumstances and had no objection to my leaving. On Saturday night being the week before Christmas (December 17th) he paid me my wages and a small balance on account of overtime due to me and we parted very good friends indeed.

I proceeded home to Hoo, for a week's holiday before commencing my new duties, and spent a very happy holiday, being frequently visited by the young woman before mentioned, (Miss A.C. Smith) who by her conversation and manners showed a great attachment to me. I, once during my stay paid a visit with my father to her home when she still seemed very anxious about my welfare and on the day of my departure from Hoo, she came twice to see me (it being on a Sunday) and the last time left a note for me - which I did not open till I was some distance on the road. This I answered after I arrived in London and very shortly afterwards I received another long letter from her in which she confessed her attachment to me and proved to me how sincere her love was for me, and in very pathetic language entreated me to accept her hand and heart, in fact, all she had even to her life itself "for" she said "if I do not marry <u>you</u>, I will die an old maid and <u>never</u> marry at all - nevertheless, I am willing to wait as long as you deem right and proper and expedient for such a consummation of my love for you":- she concluded earnestly begging me not to be offended at her boldness and plainness of speech, for, she could no longer refrain from unburdening her breast and heart of that load of pent-up - unexpressed love and affection for me, which had been gradually increasing up to that time from the moment it had commenced, and that was, from the day that we were both confirmed in the village church of High Halstow. This I answered in a manner very satisfactory to her feelings and without reserve accepted her proposals.

Chapter 8th

The Electric Telegraph Company's Office is in Lothbury behind the Bank of England. Altho they have numerous other offices, this one is the chief of the metropolitan offices and in fact of all the stations in the Company. It is as it were the centre of the Company, here all orders, rules and regulations are issued, and all the accounts received examined and passed, to this place the whole of the stations forward at intervals of 2 or 3 days all the messages received by them together with an abstract of them all. The whole management of this Company's business is carried on here = It is in this place that all the lines of telegraph in the United Kingdom and from the Continent radiate into one common centre - hence the distinctive appellation of "Central Station" is derived and given to the Lothbury Station.

Views outside and inside the Electric Telegraph offices at Founders Court, Lothbury as might have been observed by the author

The Building in itself is a very extensive one, it consists of a large hall open up to the skylight - this is approached by a narrow passage called "Founder's Court". in front over the doorway may be seen the large clock worked by electricity. On attaining the interior of the 'hall' immediately before you may be seen the Committee Room - on the left a flight of stairs - leading to different departments on the different floors, some devoted to

Examination of papers, messages, accounts and other to instrumental operations, forwarding and receiving the messages = Another department is occupied in making up "Expresses" and supplying "Press Intelligence", this is called the Intelligence Department = On the right of the entrance behind the counter (which extends round two sides of the hall) is situated the "Code Room", the Superintendent's office and immediately over this is the Secretary's Office and other Departments, the highest of which is used for instrumental work. The messages on either side are raised from the Counter to the Instrument Room by means of a "lift" which consists of a wooden square tube divided into two parts - a wheel and windlass handle placed at the top over which passes a rope furnished at each end with a square box - so that when one box is at the top the other is at the bottom and vice versa. A signal is given to draw up or put down the messages by means of a small bell. and communication is held from top to bottom & vice versa by means of a gutta percha speaking tube. The whole establishment is carried on by strict order and discipline and every different Department has its own description of employment. Under the building is a large cellar where the batteries, acid, etc etc are kept. The broken instruments or those found defective are repaired on the premises. From the foregoing will be conjectured that this station does an immense business in all departments and I assure any reader that such is really the case. Messages to and from all parts of the kingdom and the Continent are continually passing through this office. In order to ensure the greatest accuracy in the time of all stations and that as all the messages are timed on being forwarded received or transmitted in order to avoid any discrepancy in the time, every morning at ten o'clock a current of electricity is sent from Greenwich Observatory which causes a ball to fall at Lothbury and this current is also communicated to the principal stations in the country at the same moment and these again communicated by a very simple contrivance to all the minor stations, and thus every station may be warned every morning when by Greenwich time it is exactly ten o'clock. Those clocks that are wrong are corrected immediately and thus all the clocks throughout the Company's whole lines are all exactly right by Greenwich time. With such rapidity & expedition is this "time current" transmitted that from

Greenwich to Edinburgh or Glasgow there is scarcely two seconds of time lost, and that occurs merely in giving the "word of mouth at the time the ball falls at Lothbury. In the establishment there is a Room set apart entirely for "learners" in which are connected up in the usual manner instruments in pairs, one representing the sending station's instruments and the other that of the receiving station. Thus "learners" are enabled to hold conversation with each other in the same room the same as in the instrument rooms the clerks hold communications with stations hundred of miles distant. This "Learners Gallery" (as it was termed) contained two pairs of "Needle Instruments and one pair of "Printing Instruments at the time that I entered as a "Learner" which was on the 27th day of December 1852. Well knowing that I should receive no wages till I was competent to work the instruments tolerably well and being very short of funds, I resolved to work as hard as I could at them in order that I might in the shortest possible time be prepared to pass my examination.

Double and single needle instruments as might have been used by the author

I strove hard and in a few days I became so far initiated in it that by Double Needle I could read on an average about 5 or 6 words per minute. At the end of the first week I could read 10 words per minute. From 10 to 12 being the required complement to pass my examination I left that and commenced the second week with single needle. In this I progressed very rapidly and occasionally practised the Double Needle. At the end of the second week I was prepared to pass the examination which I have since known some learners to be studying for 3 or even 6 months, viz to read 12 words double and 6 words single per minute. I sent in my request to be examined. As there were no more ready the Examiner would not examine one that week but said I must wait till the following week, when some more could be ready, and in the meantime I was to learn the Printing Telegraph. This I set about with the same spirit and by dint of perseverance I was able to read and send tolerably by printing at the end of the third week, when having successfully passed my examination in the Double and Single Needle I was removed from the "Learner's Gallery" into the "East Gallery" or Instrument Room. On entering this Department I was appointed "writer" to the Manchester Printing Instruments. The complication of "codes" of different kinds puzzled me at first but in 2 or 3 days they began to be familiar and I got on very well. My Superintendent made frequent enquiries as to which progress I was making with the Printing as he said, "I shall want to sent you away to Southampton to open the printing Telegraph between that place and London in a week or two and you will be stationed there". I accordingly endeavoured to make as rapid progress as I possibly could in the little time I had, for the Instrument was generally occupied incessantly from about 9am till I left in the afternoon my duty being from 8am till 5pm. but by writing so many messages I got thoroughly initiated with the mode of sending the messages and learned numerous codes more particularly necessary and in very few leisure moments reading from the "slips" the messages that had been received thus getting as much practice as I possibly could under the circumstances. I had not been in this Instrument Room more than 3 weeks before I received notice that I was to prepare to go to Southampton on the following day the 17 day of February 1853, the new printing wire between London and that place having now been completed. Accordingly I packed up and started on my journey by the 1pm o'clock train from Waterloo Bridge Station on the abovementioned day and arrived in Southampton about 4 o'clock. Having reported myself to the Superintendent I went to look for lodgings. These I found to be very high indeed and I was compelled to accept the first I could obtain (they being very scarce) at 5/= per week* for room and attendance. Here I lived very comfortably. My salary on passing my examination commenced at 14/= per week, but on being sent to Southampton I was allowed 3/= per week "subsistence money" until such time as I should be appointed on the regular staff of the Station. Some days elapsed from the date of my arrival before we obtained the little necessaries in order to commence operations with the Printing Telegraph. I cannot but reflect upon the responsible situation I then held = sent down to this place as sole printing clerk. no-one else being in the office or within a distance of 80 miles who could read or send by this instrument and I had only sent about 4 messages and received a like number while in London therefore could not boast of being very proficient at it myself and should I break down I had no-one to assist me in any manner. Thus was I situated at the time that all the requisites were received from London and all ready to begin practical operations. My success in working this Instrument far exceeded my anticipations and I found that with plenty of patient practice and perseverance I should very soon become proficient. I continued to give general satisfaction and had sole charge of that department for a long time. In course of a few months some of the other clerks had learned it and were able to relieve me occasionally. Our office at that time was approached by a door opening from the Railway Station platform, thence up a flight of stairs, but a more dirty incommodious and inconvenient place I never saw that was this office = The business increasing it was necessary to have another built, which was in front of the Railway Station opening from the road, much more conveniently situated and much more commodious, yet not perfection for many things with some expense might have been differently made and have been more convenient and comfortable for the clerks. However it was a vast improvement upon the old one. We entered our new office on 22 June 1853. Our Clerk-in-Charge was a very disagreeable personage for, do whatever one might for him he never appeared

---

* 5 shillings is 25p in modern currency. [Eds]

satisfied. He and I could not agree at all, for he neglected his duty so much leaving the business in the hands of myself or some other clerk and went out himself taking his pleasure = I knowing this to be very injurious and derogatory to Company's interests and in consideration of and conformity with the Agreement and Conditions of Service signed by me at the commencement of my service in the Company acquainted headquarters with the circumstances of the case, and in due course he was removed and another sent in his place. This occurred in July 1854. In consequence of the Landlady of the house where I was living having taken another house I was compelled in November 1853 to change my place of abode and accordingly went to live in West Front about 1/2 a mile from the office. Here I lived very comfortably and at much less expense than in my previous lodging, thus enabling me to replenish my stock of clothes which was then pretty nearly exhausted. I was in October 1853 appointed on the regular staff of the Southampton Station at a salary of 17/= per week and 3/= p. wk "subsistence money" was then taken off, leaving my real income the same as before. Soon after this a new wire was erected between London and Portsmouth for the purpose of carrying on direct communication instead of (as previously) sending all messages via Southampton. Accordingly I was appointed to go down to Portsmouth to open this line of Telegraph which I did and the result of the first communication direct with London was very satisfactory.

On the last day of May 1854 the line of Telegraph from Lymington, Hants was extended to Hurst Castle en route to Cowes and Osborne House Isle of Wight. At this time the King of Portugal was hourly expected on a visit to Her Most Gracious Majesty Queen Victoria and a request was made from Buckingham Palace that as the wires were completed as far as Hurst Castle - some competent person should be sent there in order to watch for the King's vessels passing the "Needles Passage" and to signal the fact immediately to Southampton thence to be conveyed to Buckingham Palace. I was the party chosen for this purpose and accordingly proceeded upon my way to Lymington on the evening of the 1st of June 1854. Arriving there, I made my way to the office there which I found, and having taken a copy of the Portuguese Royal Standard from a signalling book I went home with the clerk for the night, having had supper we went to bed & rose early next morning about half past five and he went with me about 2 or 3 miles on the way to Hurst Castle, when he bade me "goodbye & I proceeded alone. Being so early we had no breakfast before we started and by the time I reached a small place called "Keyhaven" I began to feel rather hungry: this was about 7.0am. I saw about one public house & no shops & even that was closely locked up - I saw no-one about anywhere - I accordingly went on a little further & came to a small farmyard - here I stood looking at the fowls and cattle, when I saw a man come out of the cowhouse and entering into conversation with him he asked me into the house = I went in & he told me to help myself to bread and cheese and new milk which was just then very acceptable and I made a very hearty breakfast, after which I proceeded on my journey again round the shingle bank composed of the sands and loose stones, into which, when walking, one sinks up to their knees and it is very hard work to make any progress at all - however the tide being low and sands dry I managed by walking on them close by the water's edge, to make very good progress, and by 9o'clock I had reached the Castle. I happened of a Coast Guard close by, who took me to the Sergeant's house, in the Barracks, where the key of the office had been left. having obtained it I proceeded to the office & found it in a very curious plight = it consisted of two rooms. The entrance was by a porch & front doors leading to the Instrument Room or office and the inner room was intended for a Bedroom = In the first of these were the following articles: under the window a carpenter's bench upon which were some old planks & some spare slates, left after completing the roofing, on the opposite side of the room up one corner stood a very dirty wheelbarrow filled with oil cans, paint pots & brushes - a line seive - nail bags & sundry other articles & upon the floor were some coils of spare wire, tar pots &. &. in the other corner was fitted a cupboard on the top of which was placed the Instrument. There was a fireplace but no fender or fire irons or fuel = not a stool or a chair to sit down upon. The inner room was empty with the exception of a ladder & a few pieces of flooring. Thus found I the office at Hurst Castle on my arrival. There was at a little distance a "canteen" for the soldiers & men working at the castle &.

Two views of Hurst Castle. The picture at the top shows the castle as it was before the extensions which were carried out between 1852 and 1856 at a cost of £6,725 (Palmerstown's follies). The spit of land by which the author might have approached the fort on foot can be seen in the lower picture.

I repaired thither to see what I could get to eat for I began to want something a little more substantial than bread and cheese. I found that I could purchase nothing in this isolated place but eggs and bacon so during all my stay I had to live upon "eggs and "bacon". I partook of them & then repaired to the office = I soon got some visitors from amongst the soldiers who were very curious to "see the Telegraph worked". Evening came on and it began to get cold & dark - One of the soldier's wives supplied me with a candle & firing and as I had nothing to lie upon to rest myself one of the soldiers (who was on watch) brought me his mattress & blankets & we spread them on the floor and made a very comfortable bed - but fearing lest the ships (three in number) should arrive during the night I was fearful of going to sleep = and thus I lay down merely to rest my body getting up occasionally to look out and to attend to my fire. I had made arrangement with the Coast Guard and the soldier on duty to call me if they should happen to see them coming however they did not make their appearance before the third day after my arrival, during which time I had not had one hour's good sound sleep = At length the vessels hove in sight the three forming a triangle. The "Missidello" on board of which was the King of Portugal, was in front & the Saldanah & the other were close behind = I accordingly signalled them and reported their arrival to Southampton, thence it was immediately forwarded to Buckingham Palace & other places & having performed my duty I on the following morning went with three soldiers in the post boat to Keyhaven thence on foot with them to Lymingon =thence by omnibus to Brockenhurst & thence finally by rail to Southampton, this was the first opening of that Line of Telegraph beyond Lymington.

The Committee of our Company having been pleased to grant that every clerk should have a fortnight's holiday every year = I in August 1854 made application for mine & obtained my leave & the first week in September I left for a week (for being short of clerks I could not be spared longer). I proceeded to Hoo to spend a few days and the remaining few days I spend at Clandon with my parents who by the bye had left Hoo and were holding a School at this place near Guildford. In November 1854,the weather becoming very cold and it being a very dreary walk to West Front I resolved to change my residence and take up my abode close by the office in the house of a Mr Simmons who was thoroughly conversant with the French Language as was also his wife & I thought that by living with them I might be enabled to gain a knowledge of that language from them & as they promised to do all they could for me if I went to live with them, I resolved to do so & accordingly on the 11th of Nov. I left West Front and went to live in Orchard Terrace - Here I lived for a long time, but I cannot say I was so comfortable as I had been previously for here were a number of children, none of whom appeared to know how to conduct themselves properly but were the most unruly, self-willed, disobedient children I ever met with in all my scholastic experience. As for obtaining any practice in French, that was out of the question, for Mr S. had obtained employment in the Docks and was by his duties generally away from home, and Mrs S. was too much engaged with her family, school and domestic duties to spend any time to practice conversation with me - in fact instead of applying myself to it more earnestly I did not pursue it half as much as I had previously done. The prospect of getting more practice in this Language and in the practice of the pianoforte were the two principal causes of my changing my last lodging, having spoken to Mrs S. in reference to receiving musing lessons from her, but never having come to terms, I thought no more of it - as after receiving two lessons she was taken ill and laid up for several weeks, thus breaking off my lessons altogether. Time rolled on and in April 1855 I was offered a promotion to the New Station opened in the Clarence Yard Gosport, under the Admiralty, but considering the prospects I had at Southampton & the fact that together with overtime I had an income of more than the promotion would equal - I declined the offer preferring to remain and take my chance at Southampton. In due course my turn came for promotion and on the fourth of August 1855 I was promoted to a salary of one pound per week.

> Editors' note
> There is a section in the authors Technical Autobiography which it is believed the author started some later than this document. It contains a section which describes some personal experiences from about this time and for that reason the editors have added it here as indented text.
>
> " . . . .but this experience did not deter me from joining in a party for delivering a government telegram at Osborne House, Isle of Wight, which came to the Southampton office late one evening.

Osborne House, Isle of Wight (summer home and retreat for Victoria and Albert)

This necessitated the hiring of a sailing boat, and making sail for Cowes, and three of us kept each other company on this occasion besides the boat's crew. It was a very dark night and the light at Calshot Castle appeared all the more vivid as we sailed past it - we reached Cowes safely and with our precious telegram groped our way through the streets and along the road to the gate of the grounds belonging to the Palace. "Who goes there?" demanded the guard at the gate and this led to an explanation which was sufficient to admit us inside the guarded territory. It was too dark to see road of footpath and the only guide we had was a dim light in one of the palace windows for which we shaped our course in a direct line. What we crossed before we reached the house, we never knew - it might have been road, footpath, lawn or flowerbeds, all were the same colour in the darkness of the night, but a great variety appeared to pass under our feet in this straight course to the goal for which we made.

Having reached the wall of the house the next thing was to find a door, and after some searching, right and left, we did so - and then knocked - no answer. Knocked again - no one stirred. We searched for a bell pull, found one and rang - this aroused someone, a light appeared and a tall man came to the door. The usual explanations followed its opening and we were asked inside.

The message was taken to the person to whom it was addressed, and we were requested to wait for an answer. To fill up the time "((-----))" drew a can of beer, and gave us a ((horn)) mug to drink it from, but as there were no bread, cheese, or other eatables to be got, the beer did not go down very nicely alone, in the middle of a dark cold night, after a ten or twelve miles sail.

Having got our reply we left, and again took a straight course to the gate which we found after some trouble, and having passed the sentry we proceeded to find our boat. My two companions were rather boisterous gentlemen and although they had not had anything to make them particularly mischievous they persisted, in spite of remonstrances on my part, in knocking at poor inoffensive peoples' doors - ringing bells and unhinging small gates on the way down to the waterside. The perpetrators of these pranks were of course never discovered and doubtless some poor innocent victims were credited with the mischievous sport of my comrades.

We found the boat, and having got all snug we hoisted sail for Southampton and arrived safely."

Another year had rolled round since I had my last vacation & it brought me another chance of obtaining a holiday. Accordingly I made application for the same, and it was granted me - I left Southampton on 16th August and proceeded to London, stayed there a day & on the Monday I proceeded by an early train to Strood, for Hoo. On my arrival at the terminus I found Miss A.C. Smith and her sister Elizabeth waiting for me:- It having come over very wet and dull, we took a fly and proceeded to their house, where I was very welcomely greeted by their parents. Here I stayed until the following Friday:- in the meantime amusing ourselves with music and singing and daily taking a long roam about the fields and meadows = and, being harvest time, the reapers might be seen in all directions laying low the "golden grain" = stacks of wheat and other grain were rising up in all quarters and the yellow hills were speckled over with the shocks of wheat here & there interspersed with a field of beans with black sheaves giving a pleasing effect to the landscapes. In another place might be seen men in their shirtsleeves labouring and toiling with their forks pitching up the sheaves into the waggons and every now and then the impatient horses would move a few paces and were again pulled up for a few more minutes- Thus the shocks one by one would disappear and leave the field apparently empty. But is such the case? Has the apparently empty field nothing left in it? It would appear that there is something still left or why do the poor people cluster in scores round the gates and gaps and stiles anxiously & eagerly watching for the exit of the last load? Soon we have our minds satisfied upon the subject; no sooner has this load left the field than the "gleaners" with the sacks, bags, aprons & strings scatter themselves in all directions over the field, and now instead of shocks of corn we see more thickly scattered living beings moving with bended backs through every furrow and over every ridge in the field. In a little time we find a handkerchief, a bonnet, cap or some distinguishing signal laid on the ground and round it one by one the "gleans" are brought and placed like a family round the fire in winter time: - These little clusters of gleans the reward of patience and diligence are soon seen all over the field and as the time rolls on we find them slowly and still more slowly added to the others for the ears become scarce & the best corn has gone, and now the produce scarcely pays the toil and labour in procuring it: A signal arrives that another field is "cleared" - The announcement is as if aided by the magic influence of the Electric Current heard in all quarters of the field, and then we see running & bustling; mothers calling their children, children their brothers & sisters; another tying up the precious grain in a bundle and they then all following the same impulse, make the best of their way to the newly cleared field there again to repeat their operations + once more we find the formerly empty field again empty, aye still more empty than before.

"The Gleaners" by Jean-François Millais

One day we proposed visiting Cooling Castle, lying beside the banks of the Thames. The morning was very warm. We proceeded however on our intended journey, we crossed several fields at the side of which lay a thick wood in the midst of which upon branches might be heard the varied songs of the little songsters, warbling their Creator's praise. All at once a lark would start up and pursue his upward course towards the "Gate of Heaven", singing as he higher soared until he would be lost to view = and only by the sweetness & clearness of his warbling would we know of his presence above our heads. Soon however he gently sink & comes again to view & not like "the infernal serpent" whom the Almighty hurled headlong flaming from the ethereal sky with hideous ruin & combustion down to bottomless perdition there to dwell in adamantine chains and penal fire, but on downy wings he darts headlong into the ripened corn and hides himself amongst the straw:- or into the meadow of "living green" & feeds himself upon a poor unlucky worm which has dared to come out of his dark abode and enjoy the fresh air & the cool breezes which are being wafted over the face of the meadow! At length we arrived at the summit of a steep hill affording a pleasing prospect of the surrounding country. After running and jumping from mound to mound and after many an escape from slipping and falling we safely reached the valley beneath and after a little time reached the castle. We found it consisted of a very old ruin: In the interior of the walls and ravines, partly filled with water, over which were drooping some weeping willows, as if mourning over the vast change that had taken place in the scene of years gone by, stood a house, inhabited - The entrance was gained by a large gateway between the immense pillars or towers of stone - We had not time to enter the interior so passed & pursued our course in another direction & after passing several fields we came once more in sight of "home, sweet home" and soon arrived there being rather fatigued = I will not dwell longer upon this point, suffice to say that during my residence those few days at the "Deangate Cottage" I enjoyed myself as much as anyone could wish to do - plenty to eat and drink & good company = Thus the days passed very pleasantly & cheerfully = On the Friday I & the two daughters prepared for our journey to London and once more bade adieu to that pleasant spot. We arrived safely in London and on the following morning I and Ann started for Lamport to pay a visit to my Brother leaving her sister Elizabeth at her Brother Joseph's in the City. We took our tickets for Northampton and arrived there at about 12.15. My brother having met us showed us the principal objects of interest in the town during the few hours we stayed there & having sent Anne forward by a carrier's cart, I and my brother paid a visit to a Mr Daffen one of the Schoolmasters at Northampton and formerly one of our Schoolfellows at Cambridge = having spent a short time with him we proceeded on our way to walk to Lamport - distant nearly 9 miles. In due time we arrived at his home, where he made us very comfortable till Tuesday morning - during our stay we had visited all the principle objects of interest in the neighbourhood, amongst which was a visit to the gardens of Sir Charles Isham, Bart: where was the most splendid collection of flowers and shrubs I ever saw of the choicest descriptions. On Tuesday morning early Anne and I started off for a walk to Northampton on our way home = accompanied during the first few miles by my Brother, who was very loth to leave us:- We arrived safely at Northampton & ultimately found ourselves at Euston Square. The following day I, Ann and

Elizabeth went to Walthamstow, Essex, to call upon my Mother's sister = & in the evening returned to London. On the Thursday we started from Waterloo station en route to West Clandon to spend the remainder of my holiday there with my parents. Here we had a good opportunity of viewing the beauties of Nature in all its varied forms and having seen all there was to see there on the Monday following I proceeded to Southampton leaving Anne & Elizabeth to extend their visit as long as they chose. thus I spent my holiday in the most happy manner I possibly could in the harvest of 1855.

Anne Charlotte Smith

In the next chapter I will endeavour to relate a few incidents which occurred immediately after my return from my vacation, and to explain a little of the state of affairs as I found them on arriving at Southampton.

Chapter 9th

Previous to departing for my fortnight's holiday a few very unpleasant circumstances occurred between some of the Simmons family (with whom I was living) & myself, which together with the advantages I anticipated being frustrated, compelled me to think of making a change of residence, accordingly while absent upon my holiday I wrote my intentions to them with the cause. They became enraged at this and ere I returned had not failed to do their utmost to lessen me in the eyes of my District Superintendent and Clerk-in-Charge, by raising false and infamous charges against me, charging me with "betraying the confidence placed in me by my employers" and "defamation of the character of my Clerk-in-Charge" & other vile & unfounded charges, with all of which, on my entering the office, I was charged in succession = My readers can better imagine than I can describe, what were my feelings on hearing this:- protestations of my innocence were apparently vain, they appearing to have no effect for some time; I was accordingly placed upon night duty in order to be kept (as it were) out of sight from all the other clerks and looked upon with disdain as a thoroughly suspicious character;- My feelings on going on duty the first night I cannot describe & no one can imagine = for on arrival I found the door leading to the Superintendent's office (usually left unattended) sealed across from door to doorpost with a piece of red tape and sealing wax. I took this hint as a charge of dishonesty & many other infamous propensities of which I knew I was innocent: had I been the worst character that ever passed the doors of Newgate I could not have been looked upon with more suspicion, nor treated with more disdain! my heart was almost broken I knew not what to do. I shut myself up in the day almost like a prisoner and amused myself with study and writing = For ten weeks I was kept on this duty from midnight till breakfast time, and for what cause I knew not. I demanded an explanation but it was refused me thus I was compelled to submit to (I may say) persecutions for unknown offences! not only did they try to injure my character and loose my footing in the Company in which I was employed, but they most unjustly sent me a claim for two guineas for lessons in French and music which I had not received and which in fact they had promised to assist me in gratuitously and on my remonstrating with them they said that they should keep all my books, writings etc etc until I should pay the claim and if not paid they would put the matter in the County Court:- What with one thing and another I was half out of my senses, I knew not what to do, I dreaded my name appearing in the local newspaper as being summoned for a trifling thing & I agreed to pay them when I could. It was not long before I was enabled so to do - for the landlady (Mrs Durbrow) at my new lodgings, on my explaining matters to her, voluntarily offered me any amount I might require in order to get clear of them. I then settled with them & obtained my books etc. In a few weeks the prejudice which had been raised against me at the office, lacking ground of support & confirmation, soon began to decrease & I was by the assistance of the Almighty, once more placed on my former footing = And before I go further I cannot but record the great comfort and support I found in my religious exercises and devotions and reflect upon the great providence of God carrying me through all these trials and difficulties in answer to my most earnest petitions to Him!

HMS Hawke

On the 16th November my Brother Thomas having returned from the Baltic in H.M.S. Hawke, I went to Spithead to see him & having found him & obtained him leave of absence for the day I spent a very comfortable day with him.

About the middle of January 1856 Mr Neville our Clerk-in-Charge left his situation and his place was supplied by a Mr Alcock from the Company's office at Holyhead:- Not long after this the Superintendent left, his place being filled by Mr W.H. Preece a very just, upright, impartial person, a clever engineer and a man who thoroughly understood his business, in fact, just such a one as was wanted.

W.H. Preece who eventually became Chief Engineer at the Post Office

Shortly after this I began to think seriously of getting married and having consulted her with whom I had been in correspondence for about three years. I found her extremely anxious that such a favourable termination should be arrived at; and finding all friends on both sides equally agreeable to our union, the necessary arrangements were made forthwith and on the 27th day of March 1856 I was married to Miss Ann Charlotte Smith (second daughter of Richard and Elizabeth Gooding Smith of Hoo in the county of Kent in the Parish Church of St Mary Southampton. My father came and spent the propitious season with us and accompanied us on our wedding tour to the Isle of Wight where we enjoyed ourselves much indeed.

St Mary's Church, Southampton

In the month of August as usual my annual fortnight's leave of absence came round and on the 16th day of that month I and my dear wife started for our tour which was not quite so extensive as that of the previous year. We proceeded direct to Hoo and spent a week with our friends & relatives, enjoying ourselves much. At the end of the week we went to London for two days, on the second of which we went, accompanied by my Brother from Lamport, (who had come for a few days to London) to the Crystal Palace. The contents of that building I will not here attempt to describe but refer my readers to those works devoted solely to that wonderful collection of the natural and artificial productions therein amassed together and arranged for inspection = Suffice to say, we were highly delighted and amused by what we saw and after spending a whole day there we returned home in the evening quite fatigued with our day's walking. The following day I and my devoted wife with her sister Elizabeth took our journey to my parents at West Clandon & spent the remaining few days of our vacation there where we also enjoyed ourselves to our heart's content. At the expiration of which we returned to Southampton, for me, once more to resume my duties. =

Shortly after we had returned the Mastership of Hoo School becoming vacant my Father applied for the same & succeeded in obtaining it. He proceeded there forthwith.

Crystal Palace in 1856

Chapter 10th
A sudden illness, altho' of very short duration, compelled me at Christmas time 1856 to keep from my employment at the office for a few days, after which time I was again enabled to resume my duties. Not many days after this our Clerk-in-Charge having in some measure stepped beyond the bounds of prudence and for other misconduct was sent about his business to seek employment elsewhere, thereby creating a vacancy in the Clerk-in-Chargeship of the Station. The Superintendent (Mr Preece) having examined his list of Clerks found by virtue of the right of seniority that a Mr Langdon was entitled to the situation who was then in charge of our Portsea Station. This person had by most extraordinary means & good fortune been advanced most rapidly in the Company's service - so much so, that he had entered the Company only about 3 years previously & had acted as a Junior Clerk under me at the Southampton Station - from which place he was promoted to Winchester at 12/= per week, thence to Portsea at £1 - there being no other clerk at any of the smaller stations suitable to be put in charge of Portsea at the time of its becoming vacant. The business at that Station at that time was very small - but after Mr Langdon's appointment there the Russian war caused a great increase to the business of the Dockyard & Town of Portsmouth & by consequence of the Electric Telegraph Business of the Office there. The business therefore increased so rapidly that another clerk was necessary to do the business, one not being sufficient. The Directors seeing this & that the clerks got off the business very well increased the

rank of the Station and gave to Mr Langdon a promotion which placed him in point of rank next to the Clerk-in-Charge of Southampton Station - consequently, on the latter becoming vacant, he was the most entitled to it according to the Rule of Seniority & accordingly it was given him - Notwithstanding many others had been much longer in the service than he, but who, unfortunately had not been favoured with quite so many of the propitious smiles of Dame Fortune. For my own part, I could but feel annoyed and hurt to see one advanced so much before me, who had been once beneath me, when at the same time I was confident of having done my duty equally as well and equally as conscientiously as he towards my employer. I therefore wrote what I felt to my superintendent stating how it was that he was placed higher than myself who had been far the longest in the Service - with all which he was quite unacquainted and expressed to him a hop that something would ere long be done for me. He wrote me a very kind reply stating that he was "only too glad to learn of any time the feelings and sentiments of those under him" that he would do all in his power to obtain me a promotion, but it required no application on the part of those under his Superintendentship to instigate him to obtain them advancement, he considered their interests his own, and he did all he could for them, while he had at the same time the interests of his Directors to serve. - He then pointed out how his list of seniority stood, as he found it, adding that nothing that transpired between the late Superintendent and his clerks had the least influence with he, that he treated all as he found them and formed his opinion of their qualifications from their actions and exertions during the time they were under him. He hoped that no feelings of jealousy would exist between myself and Mr Langdon & that if he had been more successful that I had, I must attribute it to the fortune of life. He concluded by saying that I might quite satisfy myself upon one point - that he would pay as much attention to my interests as he would to his own and when it was in his power to promote me, he would.

I satisfied myself with this reply and not many weeks after he informed me that he had succeeded in getting me an increase of two shillings per week making my income twenty two shillings per week but not being allowed 'overtime', it was not pecuniarily speaking an increase.

I had forgotten to mention that on the 6th November 1855 I made my first début in public, having on the evening of that day delivered to the members of the Southampton Athenaeum, of which I was also a member a lecture upon "The History and Progress of Geographical Discovery" and gave general satisfaction to my audience, having an attendance of about 50 or 60 members, I was soon after elected to serve on the Committee of Management for the next six months. On New Year's 1856 we had a grand Soirée in the Trinity School Room where our Athenaeum was held and numbered about 250 present at tea. After tea was cleared away everyone present having eaten and drank to their hearts content, speeches and addresses were made by the Mayor (Sampson Payne Esq), I.R. Stebbings Esq - Rev. S.S.Pugh and other gentlemen = while between their addresses the company was highly amused by a selection of choice pieces of music - sung by three or four men & an equal number of females accompanied on the pianoforte by Mr Broads Jr. The company were also highly amused by recitations from Messrs Goodhead, Wooley and Holmes- the latter figuring most prominently in his recitation of "The Law and "The Bedpost" - The National Anthem having been sung by the entire assembly and several donations towards the Friends having been voluntarily given by the gentlemen on the platform, the meeting broke up. The room - for the occasion - was splendidly decorated with flags of all sizes and nations and many exquisite pieces of painting and calligraphy ornamented the walls, altogether the rooms presented a coup d'oeuil very pleasant and agreeable.

I was very soon after this requested by the Committee to give another lecture to which I consented and accordingly on the 1 April 1857 it was announced by handbills & placards that I would deliver a lecture on the "Means of Acquiring Information" This lecture went off very well and gave thorough satisfaction to all who heard it and I have every reason to believe that the audience were one and all highly entertained & instructed.

When the days began to get a little longer I required some other recreation to occupy my mind so I joined the Southampton

Union Cricket Club and many a pleasant hour have I passed in the Antelope Cricket Ground Southampton both in practising with the members of our own club and also in witnessing matches played with our, and other clubs, with those of the surrounding villages & towns. On the 7th July 1856 I was chosen to play in the ????* Match between our club and the Oddfellows of Lymington but unfortunately the weather was so unpropitious, having rained all day that the match could not be played. The practising season of 1857 soon came round and there the noble game was resumed by us but not before I was desired by the Secretary & others to deliver to the members of our club and their friends a lecture on the 'Sports and Pastimes of Merrie England" which I assented to & delivered it at our Cricketers' Club Room near the Cricket Ground:- In consequence of my being sent about by the Electric and International Telegraph Company (my employers) to do so many different places I was deprived very much of my practice in the Game but perhaps the changes of air & scenery did me as much sanitary good as my exercise at cricket at home would have done. My ramifications were in the Spring to the Spring Meeting of Racing Horses at Epsom Grand Stand = when the Metropolitan Stakes & other races were ran. Here I enjoyed the change of air and scenery very much being the first time I have ever seen a horse race. I was highly amused with the running & the life in the betting ring, nor was I less so with the thimble riggers and card sharpers who were ever on the alert for green countrymen to lighten of their hard cash and the latter were very eager to increase the contents of their purses by such an easy method, but soon found they became lighter rather than heavier.

During the General Election my services were required at Lewes whither I proceeded via Portsmouth and after having performed my necessary duties I returned via Brighton and London to Southampton.

Time rolled on very quickly and it came to my time for my annual fortnights vacation which I applied for to commence on the first week in August but on account of the Brighton Races

---

* completely illegible [Eds]

coming off just at that time my services were required at Portsmouth during the time the clerk from Portsmouth proceeded to Brighton. I left for Portsmouth on the 4th August 1857 (my birthday) and on the evening of the 6th I received orders to proceed to the Isle of Wight, their Imperial Highnesses the Emperor and Empress of the French having arrived at Osborne on a visit to Her Most Gracious Majesty Queen Victoria that morning. I arrived there in the evening and remained until the day after their departure for St Cloud, having been on duty 20 hours per day during their stay at Osbourne. Nearly all the correspondence was carried on either in cypher or French and I being the only clerk in the District who had any knowledge of that language was chosen to go on that account. I am happy to be able to state that the despatches went off well and that it was a means of bringing my abilities in the "printing telegraph" before the notice of the Directors in London, they having at the recommendation of the Engineer (Mr C.F. Varley) awarded me a bonus of one pound "for my proficiency". The monthly return of punishments, errors, &c, &c sent for signature by all clerks in the District had the following note attached to it by the Superintendent "Mr Graves has been rewarded for the extreme care shown in his printing - the regularity of his spacing - the lengths of his dots - his rapidity in sending the acknowledgements - the absence of any useless remarks in transmitting his work and <u>above all his knowledge of French</u> - signed W.H. Preece Supt". This, as my readers may naturally suppose, was, to me, very satisfactory.

Emperor Napoleon III, Empress Eugénie and their only child, Napoléon Eugène Louis Jean Joseph Bonaparte

Chapter 11th

During the time I was at Portsmouth I received the gratifying intelligence that my dear wife had given birth to a son and heir at ten minutes before eleven o'clock on the evening of the 5th day of August 1857 and I am happy to say she got over her trouble very nicely and the child grew very fast. Who but a parent can tell the new feelings which involuntarily spring up in the breast of a father and mother when they behold before them and press to their bosom their own flesh and blood in the shape of a dear little darling!. True enough it is that children bring love with them for I now speak from experience and really I think that it makes a man love his wife and the wife her husband with such a kind of love that they never felt before and which nothing could subdue.

On my return from the Isle of Wight I went for part of my holiday & having spent a week with my friends at Hoo, I returned to Southampton bringing with me my younger brother Edward* for whom I had obtained a situation in the office. The day after my return from Hoo, viz the 26th August I was despatched to Portsmouth for a fortnight during which time nothing of particular interest transpired = I then had my remaining weeks holiday - which I spent at home in quietness with my beloved wife and darling child and did what I could to make the home, if possible, more comfortable and on the Wednesday morning September 16th I returned to my duties in the office at Southampton having been from it nearly six weeks. I found all things going on very smoothly and everything very comfortable on my return to duty.

In consequence of the Electric and International Telegraph Company entering into an arrangement with the Provident Clerks Mutual Insurance Association - and considering that "in the midst of life we are in Death" and as a means of providing for my wife and family in case I should be suddenly called to a bed of sickness or death, I (in February 1857) had insured my life in the above association. As the Directors of the Telegraph

---

* Edward Graves eventually joined the Indo-European Telegraph Co and in 1897 was murdered by natives, while inspecting the lines in Persian Baluchistan. [Eds]

Company liberally offered to their employees, by their arrangement to pay from 1/3 to 1/2 of the premiums of those clerks who consented to participate in the advantages offered, it of course then cost me and them a very small pecuniary outlay in order to ensure very great and important advantages & benefits in case of need - but thanks to the Great Physician, I have been blessed with good health and have not yet needed its assistance - certainly I cannot tell how soon I may require it.

On the last day of September 1857, the winding up for the season of the Union Cricket Club took place, and after a very friendly game during the day between the married and single members of the Club, they with their friends (numbering about sixty) sat down to a splendid dinner which had been prepared for them by the hostess of the Antelope Inn (Mrs Brooks) in our Club Room - but whilst preparing to take my place at the table to participate in the substantial viands and delicacies of the repast, I was summoned at once to go and see the District superintendent (Mr Preece) at the Office - I went and on arriving there I found that, in consequence of my knowledge of the French Language, I was to be removed to London to be appointed to a vacancy in the Foreign or Continental Department and that I was to go in a day or two. I made an apology to him, stating how I was at that moment situated and what kind of society I had left a few minutes before & requested him to excuse me, and I would meet him in the morning - "My good fellow", said he, "if I had known such was the case I would not have sent for you, be off again and enjoy yourself" - I thanked him and returned to my Club Room, where I arrived in time to see the havoc my comrades had been making amongst the dishes & and their contents, for I perceived at the first coup-d'oeuil that there remained some naked beef bones, mutton bones, some greatly reduced ham, empty vegetable dishes, skeletons of fowls in several places, a few sections of some spherical bodies rather darkly coloured, which convinced me that they had been plum puddings, and other debris being the residue after an attack made upon the originals by so powerful an array of hungry cricketers whose appetites have been sharpened by the exercise of the day and who upon entering the dining room felt in pretty good trim to do justice to what was set before them.

The remains beforementioned were in the act of being transported to the lower regions of the house, whence a short time before they had despatched full, fat and well-liking. Seeing that I had little chance of doing justice up stairs, I found my way into the kitchen and there enjoyed the good things of this world to my heart's content & after fully appeasing my appetite I went up stairs to my companions who were just finishing the last few pieces of salad left on the table.

After the table was cleared, we enjoyed ourselves amazingly by speechifying upon the rise, progress and present position of our Club, upon the abilities of our Patrons and leaders & upon the promising future career of some of the junior members of the Club - During the intervals between the speeches we were entertained by a small party of vocalists who attended for that purpose, and with toasts to Her Majesty, The Prince Consort, the Royal Family & not forgetting "Success to the Union and its components" which I assure my readers was drank with the utmost enthusiasm, Mr Green (one of our Honorary Members) as he was annually wont to do - then awarded a bat to the best batsman, and another to the best bowler for the season as an encouragement to the members of the club to improve.

The benefits I derived from the Club in the shape of social society and friendly intercourse with my fellow members (although alas doomed to be shortlived) was incalculable and I cannot leave this subject without stating that I believe the Noble Game of Cricket to be the best game in existence for invigorating the system & spreading friendship amongst all classes of society - and I cannot but add in the words of our worthy Secretary (Mr A. Dyer) while speaking upon this subject: that it "has had a very beneficial influence upon the British National Character - of the many millions composing the human race, few, if indeed any, are entirely free from cares of some sort or othe, and their effects are too often witnessed in the cadaverous cheek - the sunken eye & the attenuated limbs, but, when the unvariable attachment to the Sports incidental to the land of our birth is awakened, and means are provided for their exercise, these quickly vanish and are replaced by the bright glow, the cheerful glance and the sinewy form of robust health. Content mantles every countenance, dissipation is banished, and men of all ranks and stations become convinced that such pastimes are the germs of sound morality & permanent happiness - of national prosperity, and of national honour.

"When the "titled man of high estate" seeks refuge, in his hours of despondency, in the invigorating diversions of his tenantry, and, by joining his dependants in exciting pleasures of our English pastimes, ascertains and participates in their hopes, their feelings and their aspirations, he becomes at once a wiser and better man. His bosom is lightened, his mental and bodily faculties strengthened, and his views of men and manners expanded. The sturdy yeoman takes delight in following his salutary examples, and the poor instead of confining themselves, after the occupations of the day, to the comparatively narrow limits, and their creature comforts of home, are induced to seek enjoyment in the green fields and meadows, where they are enabled to inhale the pure atmosphere of Heaven, and to partake in a manly and healthy exercise - thus improving the condition of society - mentally, morally and physically - which must be productive of equal benefit to the employer and the employed".

On the 3rd day of October I left Southampton for London, but on arrival, finding I was not required for a few days I returned and got my goods ready & removed them, my wife and child to London. I left my brother Edward in comfortable lodgings in Southampton to shift for himself as best he could.

At the Foreign Department I found the system of working the telegraph to be quite different from the general English System - the greater part of the Instrumental Enquiries being carried on in the German language between the clerks - and I found it absolutely necessary to study a little German; but where the clerks with whom I was corresponding could not speak English, I generally made myself understood by speaking French - thus I got on very well until I picked up sufficient German to be able to ask what I wanted and to answer questions when asked in that language. After a short time I became conversant with the different style of working and became proficient at it. We sometimes communicated with very long distances - It was a frequent occurrence to speak direct with Hamburg, Berlin, Vienna, Triest, Stettin, Petersburg, Moscow & once we spoke as far at Kiev (Kief) in central Russia.

On the 2nd May 1858 the first signals were received through from and to Constantinople direct - and after half an hours conversation in French the "Directeur" on Duty there said he should lay the same before the British Minister in Constantinople, who together with the Sultan would be glad to hear the first communication having been sent and received, to and from England being the first time any signal had been transmitted ("outre manche") beyond the Channel.

On the 30th of the same month we again succeeded in repeating the experiment. Working with Petersburg is of very frequent occurrence.

A few months after I have been removed to London it was rumoured that there was an intention among speculators to form in conjunction with the monied men of the Channel Islands, a line of Submarine Telegraph from England to these Islands (vis Jersey, Guernsey and Alderney and after a time it was said that the shares had already began to be taken up - So the matter rested and nothing more was heard of it for some time.

Female staff at the Electric & International Office in Telegraph Street ca 1859

About this time I made several endeavours to get my wife's sister, Elizabeth a situation in London - and as the Electric Telegraph Company employed a great number of females at Lothbury in the English Department I thought of getting her in there, and after delay and some difficulty I succeeded. She was very comfortable and much liked by all her fellow employees - but, sad to relate - she had not been there many months when she was taken with a bad foot, which compelled her to keep her bed - and, poor girl! she has done so ever since until now (Nov. 26,'58) her foot having almost mortified away - several pieces of bone having been taken from it. Thus, she, poor suffering creature, was compelled to resign her situation, where she was respected and beloved by all who knew her*.

Things went on very comfortably with me at Lothbury. I soon became respected by those around me, and found much more to do than I had done at Southampton, which was a change I approved rather than the contrary. I obtained more society in the office among people of more advanced years and intelligence than I had done - and I liked the change as far as the office work was concerned very much - but we found lodgings very expensive and very inconvenient and uncomfortable in London. There was one thing, however attached to the office duties which I did not like much and that was, I had to take my turn at night duty one week out of every four from Midnight to nine o'clock in the morning.

During one of these lonely, dreary duties in the month of February I gave vent to my meandering thoughts in the following plaintive lines

> To work at night oft falls my lot
> And certain tis I like it not
> Yet still it must be done-

---

* A memorial inscription at Hoo St. Werburgh says " . . . also of Elizabeth Gooding Smith beloved daughter of the above named Richard Smith who departed this life on her 31st birthday December 31st 1870 after 13 years of unparalleled suffering born with the most exemplary patience, faith, fortitude and Christian endurance." We conjecture that the cause may have been bone tuberculosis. [Eds]

Complaining is no use at all
For to my lot twill often fall
    Altho' it is no fun.
So as the "witching hour" draws near
I march from home quite free from fear
    Not thinking of dislikes
In fifteen minutes I attain
The door, where I an entrance gain
    Just as (**XII**) the midnight strikes

My prospect from my window is
No other earthly thing than this
    A graveyard - cheerless - grim!
The stones in which are near decay
Some very old - the people say
    Plac'd over her, or him.
But darkness almost shrouds the scene
And what those inmates may have been
    I muse upon alone
When all at once the calm is broke
A bell is struck with heavy stroke
    The neighbouring clock strikes **I**.

Tis but a moment that the sound
Vibrates upon the air around
    In silence left again -
Resume my muse - I look around
No single object can be found
    To join me in my strain
So to the graveyard I return
And think - "Can I a lesson learn
    From tombstones old and new?"
Yes - think that I and all around
Must some day in the grave be found
    Like these:- The Clock strikes **II**.

Then let me live, and others too
In whatsoever we say or do
    As if God saw it all.
For we are certain he can be

Where no one else can hear or see
    Or listen to our call.
Let us then strive to please Him still
And learn to know His Holy Will
    All evil let us flee
And we shall our reward receive
In heav'n, if we will but believe
    In Him:- The Clock strikes **III**.

My occupation I may call
Of man's inventions - "lord of all"
    Th' Electric Telegraph
What wonders daily are reveal'd
From nearly all the world conceal'd
    At least from more than half.
For few there are who know full well
How we our hidden wonders tell
    With speed ne'er known before!

'Twould volumes fill to tell the tale
Of lightning's freaks o'er hill and dale
    But hark! the clock strikes **IV**.

How grans! how most sublime the thoughts!
That man should be by Providence taught
    Th'Elements to control!!
And make the lightning at his will
Speak his desires - more wondrous still
    Thesecrest of his soul!!
Yet so it is - we wield the pen
of Electricity, and then
    Our Instruments contrive
That though some thousand miles away
We write what we may wish to say
    But stay! the clock strikes **V**.

Nor distance, land nor sea can stay
The mighty pow'r - which many say
    They scarcely can believe
The lightning speeds at our commands

To any place - where Agent stands
    In silence to receive.
A Novice loling on might say
"Why move your 'Key' in such a way
    You're only planing tricks?"
"Nay, nay, good friend, the effect you'll see
If only patient you will be"
    Hark! Hark! - the Clock strikes **VI**.

No sooner have we ceased to 'play'
As Novice thinks "in such a way"
    Than answer comes to say
The Clerk at other end of wire
Has all the telegram entire
    Our friend stares with dismay!
What I have said, my friend, to you
Is every word of it as true
    As Sun is in the Heaven
So doubt it not - for on my word
I've told you what I've seen and heard
    The Clock is striking **VII**.

The morning breaks, the sun shines bright
And clears away the gloom of night
    Which o'er the place was seen
The larks, no doubt are soaring high
Altho' not t'wards a London sky
    But where the grass is green
How pleasant 'tis - and how sublime
To hear the birds in sweet spring-time
    Their morning tales relate
And into song burst forth at times
Some hours before the Village chimes
    Denote - 'tis striking **VIII**.

My last hour's duty is begun
The golden - cheerful - looking sun
    Is rising all serene
Dispensing all the darkness quite
And making all the places light

> Oh! what a glorious scene!
> My wonderworking wires I'll leave
> The Clerk who comes me to relieve
> Appears:- Oh sight divine!
> Into the open air I come
> And then begin my journey home
> Just as the Clock Stikes **IX**.

========================

About the month of July it was evidently settled respecting the formation of the "Channel Islands Electric Telegraph Company" for officers were chosen and a contract entered into with Messrs Newall & Sons to make, lay down and hand over, a cable, in good working order by the end of July - which was accomplished and clerks were chosen to go to the different islands where stations were proposed to be established viz, at Jersey, Guernsey & Alderney - I was chosen to go to Jersey, being the chief island in the Channel.

===

Chapter 12th
I received orders to go to Jersey on the 3rd day of August 1858 to assist in signalling during the laying down of the Cable, but on arrival there I found that the Contractors had supplied their own signal clerks for that purpose. I accordingly returned to London the following day (my 25th birthday) which I spent in the following manner. I rose at five in the morning - breakfasted - & then went on board the mail packet "Courier" which sailed for Southampton at 6 o'clock = After a rather rough passage we arrived safely at Southampton & having got our Steamer alongside the Quay opposite the Customs Searching Department we proceeded to land - Then followed a scene which I had never before witnessed, for be it remembered I had never, before this voyage to Jersey, quitted my native shores, and had therefore, never arrived in England from a Foreign Country, and, as a natural consequence, had never undergone the ordeal of Customs.

Well, on entering this Searching Department I found it to be a very large warehouse-looking place with a row of tables down the centre. Every passenger upon landing had to file off singly and place his carpet-bag, portmanteau, or whatsoever baggage he had with him, upon, or near this long table =

What with the hubbub in French, English, and Jersey-patois, the confusion, impatience, protestations against the examinations being made so minutely, &c, &c, the scene represented a complete Babel. Here might be seen a Commercial-man, whose time to him was of great importance - There a Travelling Merchant, where time was money and delay a dead loss:- Here an elderly, but fidgety lady, who was in a "mighty flustration" for fear she would lose the train which was to convey her to London - there a fascinating young lady, who was encumbered (as what <u>young lady</u> is not in <u>these</u> days) with an almost incredible number of small packages and numerous bonnet boxes, trunks, &c, fearing to lose some of them which might perchance contain some of her indispensables, in the shape of her <u>toilette</u>, her <u>trousseau</u>, her <u>bijouterie</u>, her <u>chemiselles</u>, her most indispensable <u>jipous d'acier</u>:- Here, again, might be seen my humble self with my small carpet-bag, particularly waiting for my turn to pass through the examination; & there might be seen a poor soldier, handcuffed, being led away by two others, bayonets fixed, and also the receding passengers as they passed one by one out of the building into the Dock Yard having undergone their ordeal.

While I was thus awaiting my turn I was enabled to take a survey of the rest of my fellow passengers, and to observe how they got through their examinations. The Commercial-man might be observed urging the searchers to attend to him, and being quietly told to wait his turn, for be it observed, that during all the confusion, the searchers preserved a calmness and apparent natural presence of mind, patience and endurance the most praiseworthy. The Travelling Merchant in spite of protests and representations that his time was money, and delay a dead loss, being told very calmly to wait with patience:- The fidgety old lady, notwithstanding her exclamations "I'm sure I shall miss the train. I shall be too late. Hark! there's the whistle and these people are keeping me here, what shall I do? oh dear, oh dear, what shall I do?" being quieted by "my good woman, we can't favor anyone - first come first served". The young lady might be observed with her host of packages (having got them all together) modestly waiting with patience until her time came, Knowing, I presume, that they will take a long time to examine and that her time is not so precious as that of others. My own turn coming at length - the searcher feels the contents - takes a cursory glance at them & dismisses me by chalking a hieroglyphic on the bottom of it which was the sign for the doorkeeper to allow me to pass.

Having got 'cleared of the Customs' I proceeded to the Railway Station and left Southampton by the 7.15pm train and arrived in London at 10 o'clock. I immediately proceeded to my own home which I found empty of inmates (my wife & child having gone to Hoo during my expected stay in Jersey. We returned to London in a day or two and got our things packed up according to orders, and anxiously awaited, day after day, final orders to proceed to Jersey; but alas! for the dependence to be placed on man! We were kept just a week more and received no orders, so I asked, under those circumstances, to be allowed to go into the country and take my usual annual holiday, or so much of it as I could until I was really required to start. I received permission &

accordingly went again to Hoo, being given to understand that I might depend upon a fortnight as the land wires took a long time to lay down in consequence of the islands being so very rocky- I remained with my wife & child at Hoo about a fortnight during which time I amused myself much under the trees in the Orchard by carefully reading over, and making Extracts form the Wills of Richard Everist and Elizabeth Everist his widow, (being the grandparents to my wife) in virtue of which upon the death of both of her parents, she, if living- would be entitled to a share of the property. The Extracts I afterwards wrote more explicitly and have preserved them as being likely to be useful at some future time.

At the expiration of the fortnight I received orders to return to London - not to proceed thence to Jersey at once - but to resume my duty at Lothbury until required to go to my ultimate destination - the line not being in readiness for me - In this state of suspense and anxiety, living in an uncomfortable home having goods all packed ready to leave at a minute's notice, was I kept from the time of my return from Jersey on 4th of August till I received final orders to depart for Jersey on the 4th of September = On the same day I proceeded to Southampton where with my wife & child, I stayed till Monday morning the 6th & left Southampton at midnight by mail packet - bidding adieu to the favourite old town, which we were very pleased to have had the opportunity of visiting again - and where we first enjoyed the sweets of married life - where our child was born - where we had so many friends and where I had in past times spent so many, many happy hours -

We had not been long at sea before my wife, child, and myself were all taken ill with a dreadful sea-sickness, having a very rough passage, which retarded our progress so much that the steamer did not arrive in Jersey until full three hours behind her usual time under favorable circumstances - making our passage in 13 hours. I was not in very good trim myself after such a voyage - my wife was quite fatigued, worn out, and half dead and the poor little child was worse than either of us, and for several days we despaired of his getting over it - My poor dear wife vowed she would never cross the Channel again, if she never saw her parents anymore, such was the dislike she had for repeating a seavoyage of this description - but notwithstanding the rough and fatigued state I was in, I was immediately called to the Office to put the Electric Telegraph into operation and make a few preliminary arrangements and enquiries previous to the despatch of messages. On arrival at the Office (after hastily taken a little refreshment at the Hotel du Havre), I found it filled with the élite of Jersey together with the officials of the Island and town of St. Helier. The Office was literally crammed with Ladies and Gentlemen, all in anxious anticipation of the first message being transmitted across the Channel to England.

In the morning the Governor - judges - aristocracy - ministers - honorary police - and a band of soldiers formed a procession through the town, and, having paraded the principal streets, proceeding to the office - at about two o'clock, where they entered and partook of refreshments. The Governor of the Island then handed me on a crimson velvet cushion, a Message to be forwarded to Her Most Gracious Majesty Queen Victoria being the first official message forwarded to England by the new line. Her Majesty being in Scotland, the message had to be retransmitted from London, which caused it to arrive at a rather late hour in the evening at Holyrood Palace - but notwithstanding the lateness of the evening Her Majesty despatched Her reply that same night, but as we little expected to receive it that evening we closed our office, so that it was not until early next morning that we received Her most gracious reply - which gave the most heartfelt satisfaction to the whole of the inhabitants - Copies of the original message with the reply were printed, posted and circulated all over the Island and it is worthy to note, how beautifully and appropriately Her Majesty's reply was worded, being expressive of the pervious loyalty and devotedness of the Islanders and her confidence in them for the future. I have appended here a verbatim copy of the People's message together with Her Majesty's Gracious Reply to the same:- the former was Despatched and the latter received by myself.

The Message to The Queen

To the Right Honorable S.H. Walpole,
Her Majesty's Principal Secretary of State
for the Home Department.

The Directors of the Channel Islands' Telegraph Company, on behalf of the people of the Islands, solicit that you may be pleased to lay before Her Most Gracious Majesty, this the first Message conveyed by their Telegraph.

Though the establishment of this means of rapid communication with the Mother Country is an event of minor importance to the Empire at large, it is one of heartfelt satisfaction to Her Majesty's Loyal and Devoted Subjects here, — as tending to draw still closer the Bonds which for nearly One Thousand Years have linked these Islands to the Crown of England, and more firmly to secure that connection, the foundation of their Liberties and their Prosperity, and which, like their forefathers, they would deem no sacrifice too great to preserve.

Jersey, September 7th 1858.

Her Majesty's Answer

Jersey, September 8th 1858.

Earl of Derby

To The Directors of the Channel Islands' Telegraph Company, Jersey.

Holyrood Palace, Tuesday night.
7th September 1858.

The Queen has received with the highest satisfaction the announcement of the successful completion of a Telegraphic Communication with the Channel Islands; and while Her Majesty congratulates the Directors of the Channel Islands Telegraph Company upon their success, She rejoices in the more rapid means of communication and the closer connexion thus happily established with a portion of Her Dominions hitherto locally separated, but always united to Her Crown by a spirit of unswerving loyalty unsurpassed in any part of them, and of which the message just transmitted on behalf of the people of the Islands contains a very gratifying expression.

It will be seen that in addition to my having the honor of opening the line of printing telegraph from Southampton to London in the beginning of March 1853 (vide page 50*) and the printing line from Portsmouth to London in the beginning of the year 1854 (p.52**) and also the Needles Telegraph from Southampton to Hurst Castle and the Isle of Wight on the 2nd of June 1854. I

---

* in the original hand-written manuscript. This appears on p.56 in this document. [Eds]

** in the original hand-written manuscript. This appears on p. 58 in this document. [Eds]

had also the honor of opening the Line of Printing Telegraph from England to the Channel Islands, by sending and receiving the first messages on that line. I may add, also, that I was the first to work on this line direct through to London.

Scene of jubilation as witnessed by the author

The fêtes in the town of St. Heliers were carried out with a spirit of enthusiasm never before equalled - almost every street & every house vied with each other to decorate and illumine their premises the most - Flag and banners with appropriate mottoes and wreaths and garlands were stretched across the streets in every direction. In the evening the illuminations were magnificent - Bands played at Charing Cross and other places, rendered the scene most enlivening. Fire balloons were sent up at intervals from a triumphal arch at Charing Cross, and at the ascent of each vociferous cheers filled the air proceeding from the mouths of the assembled multitudes on all sides. This same evening at the Pomme d'or Hotel a Banquet was given to the Aristocracy and the Queen's Assembly Rooms another was given to "The People", every one at each place enjoying himself or herself to their heart's content.

On the 9th of September 1858 the Line was Officially opened to the public and business commenced accordingly.

The Office is situated at the corner of Church Street & Library Place, near the Royal Square and forms a corner house, the ground floor being fitted up very comfortably for the offices, and the upper part of the house appropriated for the use of the Clerks (myself and another Mr Meyer) I taking the first and he the second floor where we lived very comfortably together, after having been put to considerable expense in furnishing our portion of the house, the rooms being so much larger than any we had previously occupied, out of a limited income (altho' increased to 30/= per week[+]) we found it a long time before we could thoroughly recover this financial drawback.

View of Albert Pier, St Helier 1860. Fort Regent with its signal staff can be seen on the right

Most people in talking of the "Channel Islands" understand that term to mean nothing more than Jersey and Guernsey; and although there are few know something about Alderney and Sark (the former of which has indeed, asserted its independent existence by some very portentious figures in the annual estimates), there are not many who have so much as heard of Herm, Lihou, Ietho, Burhou, Brechou, Little Sark and the other rocks and rocklets which make up the complement of that group which, though it belongs to the English Crown - and long may it

---

[+] £1.50 in decimal currency [Eds]

do so! - lies in the Bay of Mont St Michel on the coast of Normandy. Jersey and Guernsey are of course the largest of the group - the former containing a superficies of 40,000 acres, and a population of upwards of 57,000; and the latter a superficies of 15,560 acres and a population of about 30,000. Sark is three miles and a half in length, by one and a half in breadth, and its population is about 709. It contains silver and lead mines, which have been abandoned. Herm is a little island about a mile and a half at its greatest length, and little more than half a mile at its greatest breadth. The population is not more than 30 though at one time when the quarries were worked it nearly reached 200. Iethou is a singular molehill of an islet. It is only half a mile in circumference, but can boast an excellent house. Alderney, altho' last mentioned, is not by far the less important. It is smaller than Guernsey but ranks next to it in size. Of late the enormous defensive works constructed by Government have rendered it the most important, in a political point of view, of all the islands. It is satisfactory to know, not that the mind of the country is agitated about the tremendous works which have lately been completed at Cherbourg, that upon this little island, closely watching and within ten miles of the French Coast, works are being perfected scarcely less powerful than those which have caused so much anxiety. Upon the new harbour alone, more than a million of money has already been expended, and as much more will probably be spent before it is all completed. The forts around it and upon the breakwater have also cost vast sums of money. The population in 1851 was upwards of 3,000 but it is now probably much nearer 5,000.

I have given this brief sketch of the Channel Islands in order to enable my readers to form some idea of what they are and what the prospects of the line of telegraph are likely to be. Of Jersey I may say more as I become more fully acquainted with the island myself, and am thus enabled to give more authentic information respecting it*, however in summing up a few particulars respecting the island I may just mention that its climate is very mild - natural result from its position, sloping from North to South, the northern shores being between 200 and 300 feet above the level of the sea and in some places exceeding that height - and the southern shores blending themselves to a level with the ocean, giving the island a southerly slope, and consequently rendering the climate mild & salubrious. The natural productions include apples, pears, plums, grapes, figs, apricots, peaches and all other kind of fruit, many of which would not grow to perfection in England - potatoes, turnips, carrots, parsnips, onions, rhubarb and other kitchen garden productions including cabbages for which Jersey is remarkable - the cow-cabbages in Jersey grow to from 6 to 12 feet high and look more like young trees than anything else - the stems of these cabbages are made into walking sticks which are eagerly bought by visitors as souvenirs of their visit to Jersey The first grapes &

---

* (author's footnote)

As I have devoted a separate volume to a description and faithful "Guide" to the Island of Jersey & it being too voluminous to introduce into this work I would refer my readers to that work published in Jersey in June 1859 - a copy of which will be found in the "British Museum" London.

There is an indication that Graves made the mistake of many young authors by trusting the proof-reading ability of his printers. The earliest copies have a consistent error which has been amended by hand. In the title and elsewhere, the work 'topographical' has been spelt 'typographical'. His great-great grand-son visited Jersey in 1981 and saw a copy which had been dedicated to the Editor of the Jersey Times. Through Inter-Library loan the Editors saw a copy (ILL) which had been the property of Dr Gross. A copy in the British Museum Library (BM) was also inspected. The various corrections would suggest that the Guide probably ran to three printings. [Eds]

potatoes in Covent Garden Market are almost invariably Jersey produce -

Early morning at Covent Garden Market (Gustave Doré)

The physical features of the island are a beautiful variety of hill and dale, gentle slopes and rippling streams - and verdure appearing in almost every corner of it, notwithstanding it being but one vast rock and the soil extending, on an average, but a few inches deep. The whole island is spotted with detached houses, cottages, chateaux, churches, chapels, farms, meadows, cultivated fields, and good roads leading in every direction. The distinguishing characteristics of the native inhabitants may be summarised up in a few words - Selfishness is a leading feature of the majority of the people - inquisitiveness is a predominant characteristic which pervades, I think I may say, the whole of the Jersey race - for this feature displays itself as soon as a stranger enters into conversation with any native - In the town of St Helier - pride has a large display - and dress, among the female population, whether old, young, sick or poor, seems to be the chief study, which tends to ruin a great many of the latter class, as well as the middle stage of society for an overlove of finery has so evaporated the female mind that unless it can be gratified by fair means-foul means will be resorted to obtain it, and hence the ruin of many. The poorest of the poor, appear to be determined to imitate their more wealthy superiors, and are to be seen in their wide-spread crinoline flaunting up and down as if the very ground were not fit for them to walk upon - such is the extent of this crinoline & gaudy dress mania.

If those young Ladies did but know,
Who with their wide expansive show
    of Hoops and Crinoline,
How great a laughing stock they make
For gents - they would this warning tak
    "No more in them to be seen"

Again, if those young women knew,
Who daily, nightly, hold in view
    Their mass of Crinoline,
How ev'ry man of common sense
Laughs at and ridicules th'expense
    They'd cast if off I ween,
And servant girls if they but thought
When their minds have the mania caught
    To wear the Crinoline.
How they are ridiculed by men
And laugh'd at o'er and o'er again
    They'd spurn it as unclean,

But notwithstanding what's been said
Some have been burn'e and some are dead!!
    Because of Crinoline
In spite of all the "warnings" still
The cry from females is "I will
    Still wear my Crinoline".

What pity then can be display'd
Towards those who have been begg'd and pray'd
    To give up Crinoline
When we shall hear they have been burn'd
And all their flesh in cinders turn'd

       Through wearing Crinoline!

Can we have pity for a man
Who spite of numerous warnings - can
    Himself in danger place,
When he shall in that danger fall
And when too late for help shall call
    Till he's black in the face?

What sympathy can we afford
To "Ladies" who scorn ev'ry word
    That's for their safety giv'n?
Let me with "pen and ink" then call
To females all, both great and small -
    This timely warning take:-
Put off your Crinoline, I pray,
And live in safety ev'ry day,
    I warn you for life's sake!

The subject of the foregoing lines was suggested by the extreme extravagance of the prevailing fashion, and the very numerous and fatal accidents which were occurring in consequence of the use of crinoline. But to return to my subject, The Language of Jersey is a mixture of French and English - a patois which can neither be expressed in writing, nor reduced to any grammatical rules - The Shipping of Jersey in the beginning of 1859 comprised about 430 vessels of all sizes and the commercial prospects of the island have vastly increased of late years - and are still increasing.

The first place I visited in the country was Mont Orgueille Castle - a very old building fraught with numerous historical collections for full particulars respecting which vide my "Guide to Jersey" heretofore referred to - My second excursion was to St Brelades Bay - where may be seen the Church of the parish which was consecrated in the year 1111 & is the oldest church in the island - These two excursions gave me a little insight into the beauties of the island, and inspired me with a desire to study its scenery and history - the result of these researches was the publication of my "Guide to Jersey" just mentioned.

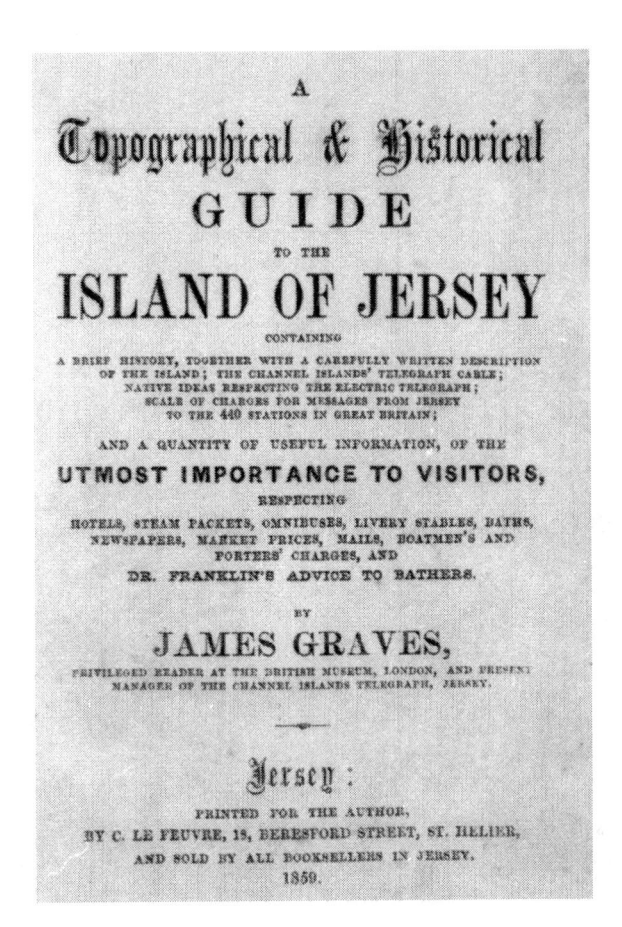

> # A
> ## Topographical & Historical
> # GUIDE
> #### TO THE
> # ISLAND OF JERSEY
> ##### CONTAINING
> A BRIEF HISTORY, TOGETHER WITH A CAREFULLY WRITTEN DESCRIPTION OF THE ISLAND; THE CHANNEL ISLANDS' TELEGRAPH CABLE; NATIVE IDEAS RESPECTING THE ELECTRIC TELEGRAPH; SCALE OF CHARGES FOR MESSAGES FROM JERSEY TO THE 440 STATIONS IN GREAT BRITAIN;
>
> AND A QUANTITY OF USEFUL INFORMATION, OF THE
> ## UTMOST IMPORTANCE TO VISITORS,
> ##### RESPECTING
> HOTELS, STEAM PACKETS, OMNIBUSES, LIVERY STABLES, BATHS, NEWSPAPERS, MARKET PRICES, MAILS, BOATMEN'S AND PORTERS' CHARGES, AND
> DR. FRANKLIN'S ADVICE TO BATHERS.
>
> BY
> ### JAMES GRAVES,
> PRIVILEGED READER AT THE BRITISH MUSEUM, LONDON, AND PRESENT MANAGER OF THE CHANNEL ISLANDS TELEGRAPH, JERSEY.
>
> ## Jersey:
> PRINTED FOR THE AUTHOR,
> BY C. LE FEUVRE, 18, BERESFORD STREET, ST. HELIER,
> AND SOLD BY ALL BOOKSELLERS IN JERSEY.
> 1859.

About this time (January 1859) I invented an Alarm Bell to be worked in conjunction with the ordinary Telegraphic instruments - for the purpose of giving the clerk notice when his machine required winding up - and thereby avoiding the inconvenience of the machine stopping in the middle of a dispatch - an advantage the value of which can only be estimated by those who by experience know the want of it. I had attached it to the machine in Jersey and found it answered admirably = I forwarded to the Engineer of the Company my drawings of it, that he might lay them before the Managing Directors - I heard subsequently that the Company intended to have some made upon the principle of my invention.

Chapter 13th
Scarcely had we got comfortably settled in our new home at Jersey than on 22nd September 1858 an order was issued in the absence of the Secretary who had appointed me - for my immediate removal to Alderney, in consequence of a more efficient Clerk being required there for testing purposes. I immediately represented the conditions upon which I accepted removal from London to Jersey, viz; that it should be permanent and was successful in getting the order cancelled on the 25th of the same month by Telegraph.

On the 1st of January 1859 my beloved wife made me a present of a New Year's Gift in the shape of a sweet daughter who was named "Edith Ann" and both mother and daughter prospered by the blessing of God, very favourably and gathered strength daily.

Not more than three or four day later than the foregoing auspicious event - a letter was received by me from the Secretary of the Channel Islands Telegraph Company, D.P Gamble Esqre to the effect that Mr Meyer, the then present Clerk in Charge & Manager at Jersey was to be removed to London and that he (the Secretary) trusted that he should never have cause to regret having recommended me to the situation thus rendered vacant. I need scarcely say that such news was exceedingly welcome as it brought with it an increase of 10/= per week in my salary*. Notwithstanding that Mr Meyer - being backed by the Local Directors in Jersey did all they possibly could to avert this change - final orders were issued, on the 8th day of January 1859, that Mr Meyer must leave and that I was to immediately assume the local management of the business at Jersey: Mr A.C. DuBois being appointed my Assistant.

I could but see in all this the finger of Providence of Him who is never faithless to promote honour those who fear & trust in Him. As was the case with me in the birth of my firstborn son, so it was with me on the birth of my first daughter. As in the former case immediately after that event my salary was increased 4/= per

---
* bringing his wages to £2 per week [Eds]

week so in the latter case I was promoted again and my salary advanced 10/= per week - thus it will be seen that he who gives us children & thereby increases our expenses also gives us the additional means whereby we can support them. Bless, therefore, the Lord, oh, our souls; and forget not all His benefits.

Thus having got comfortably settled in Jersey, and having every prospect of happiness and contentment before us, we lived in quietness at home, and in peace with all the world - but our tranquillity was doomed to be very brief and shortlived - for a letter arrived bearing date 20th January 1859, from the Secretary, the substance of which was as follows:- "Sir, It has come to my knowledge that during the time you have been at Jersey, you have conducted yourself in a most intemperate manner, assaulting a "learner" named DeDopff, and that you have also taken the same unjustifiable course with Mr DuBois your fellow clerk - he I am happy to hear rewarded you as you deserved- Now, you will clearly understand from me that a repetition of such conduct as this will involve your immediate dismissal from the service of the Company - On receipt of this you will be good enough to send me some explanation of your conduct, as at present, I must say I feel considerable doubt as to whether you are a fit person to be in the responsible position you at present hold, being unable to control your actions in a proper manner - I am, obediently yours, D.P. Gamble"-

As may be well imagined I was very much cut up upon the receipt of such a communication from him who but a few weeks previously had recommended me to the position I held, and trusted he should never regret having done so - and although I felt myself most unjustly accused, and had a clear conscience that the charge was most base and unfounded, yet I felt that upon the minds of some persons, an unfavourable impression once made, it is very difficult to make such a defence as thoroughly to eradicate it - My poor wife still confined to her bed was terribly shaken by this letter - and it was a merciful providence which kept her from a relapse which might have proved fatal.

Under these trying circumstances I placed my whole trust in Him who sees and knows all things - and who is always ready to help those out of trouble who go to Him for help. Relying upon His teaching I proceeded to the residence of Mr DeDopff - the son of a Dutch Baron - living with his Father. Having represented my position to him and his father and informing them of the charge laid against me, they were both astounded & affirmed its falsity- They immediately proceeded to write me a note in contradiction of the statements made to the following effect:-

> "Sir, Having been informed of the statement and accusation against Mr Graves, I regard it a pleasant duty to report to you that it is quite unfounded and false, for during the six weeks I have been with him at the office I always found him very polite and respectful, and his conduct gentlemanlike in all respects - Moreover if any offence had been done, I then would have communicated it to the manager in order to obtain a redress.
>
>   I remain
>   Sir
>   your obedient servant
>   Henry DeDopff -
> D.P. Gamble Esq[re]
> London."

This letter was very satisfactory to me and tended to raise my spirits a little, but to make my defence more substantial I determined to get a letter also from Mr DuBois, the other party named in the charge. He was in the country about 4 miles from St Helier, so I took a cab, and went to him, he indignantly repudiated such a charge against me and vowed it was completely false, offered immediately to contradict it & gave me the letter following:-

> "Sir,
> I think it my duty, and at the same time rendering justice to Mr Graves to inform you that since I have been in office, I have always, and in every instance found his conduct both gentlemanly and honourable towards me, and the public generally, always ready to render me any service, and doing all in his power to make me efficient in my Duty.

During the time of my learning in the Jersey Office, I firmly deny his having assaulted me in any shape or manner - Hoping you will find this testimony satisfactory, and that under Mr Graves tuition I shall render myself competent to give you every satisfaction
    I am, Sir,
            your humble & obedient servant
                      Adolphus Chevalier DuBois.
D.P. Gamble Esqre"

Having furnished myself with this evidence, without loss of time, I replied to Mr Gamble's letter by return of post in the following terms

"Dear Sir,
Language cannot express my surprise and heartfelt grief on reading the contents of your letter, charging me with intemperate conduct, and assault upon Messrs: DuBois and DeDopff - such charges being base, hardhearted, malicious, unfounded and false - and I defy the world to prove that one hour of my life has been passed in a state of intemperance or in the practice of intemperate conduct. The certificates attached will, I trust, convince you of the falsity of those charges, if my own word is not sufficiently forcible.

Trusting I shall soon her from you that your impressions respecting me have been reverse
    I am, Dear Sir,
            your obedient servant
                      James Graves
D.P. Gamble Esqre
London. "

With feelings of impatient anxiety I posted the above letters and most anxiously did I wait reply from London. My thoughts ran wildly about in all directions, searching in vain to find anyone who could have laid such a charge against me - but like Diogenes searching for an honest man, I found not one. The night passed in restlessness, and my mind's eye traced, as it were, the course of my letter on its way to London, it saw it in the Postman's hand amidst the other voluminous correspondence; it saw the whole packet sorted out into Departments after the Postman had delivered them up - it traced it to the Secretary's table - but no one there to open it, most impatiently did it watch the arrival of the man whose mind was thus turned against me; at last, he comes! letter after letter he opens and places one here, another there, another gets torn in shreds & it cast ignominiously upon the fire, or into the waste-paper basket; at last he reaches the all important one which I so anxiously had watched = he breaks the seal, unfolds the letters; reads them carefully, casts a perplexed look at the part of the contents, and thinks awhile. What means this change of countenance? my mind enquires, but patience must have its perfect work - so I am forced to wait - All at once he seizes pen & paper and writes the telegram as follows:

"Gamble London   to Graves Jersey
Your letter is satisfactory - I will write tonight"

Oh, Reader! imagine my feelings upon receipt of this brief, but effective intimation, for I cannot express them on paper, nor contemplate the feelings of my dear wife when to her bedside I brought that welcome news - think how each of our hearts leaped for joy, and how thankful we were to that Almighty Providence who had so directed my proceedings in this matte - and also enter into our anxiety to see the letter which he would "write tonight" - Most welcome was the visit of my postman on the following afternoon when he handed to me the letter which was as follows

"Dear Sir,
I have your letter, which I consider very satisfactory, as the charge was brought to me I thought it but fair that you should have the opportunity of defending yourself -

Mr DuBois (in the presence of Mr Christie one of the clerks) told my clerk, Mr Richards, that you had assaulted DeDopff and that he resigned in consequence, and that you had tried the same thing with him, but that he had knocked you down - Now I am determined to have this investigated as there must be some lying somewhere, and if you can assist me in doing this I shall be obliged to you - You will of course do this for your own sake

Trusting I shall soon hear from you that your impressions respecting me have been reversed
    I am,
           faithfully yours
                    D.P. Gamble
Mr Graves"

Upon reading this I confess I was fairly perplexed and puzzled, as well as also surprised and thunderstruck. Could it be possible that he who was now acting as my assistant, should have made such a charge against me during the time he was learning his business in London, and he who had given me a certificate emphatically repudiating such an act on my part? I could scarcely believe it. I had but one course now left me, and that was to obtain the written explanation from Mr DuBois as to the meaning of such a statement, and he must either acknowledge his guilt of a falsehood, or contradict his certificate of my innocence which he had previously handed me? I made known to him the contents of the foregoing letter and he made a thousand apologies, stated he did not remember the circumstances - and gave me a not to the following effect.

"Dear Sir,
In reply I would state that it was never my intention in any way to injure your character, or give you any annoyance it not being my disposition to lower anyone unjustly in the estimation of his superior officers - Having known me for some time I hope you will bear testimony to my having acted in quite a contrary manner. I may have mentioned something of the kind by way of a joke in a commonplace conversation with fellow clerks, but I have never had cause to make such a statement, neither did I intend them to receive it as a fact.
    I am, Dear Sir
        yours obediently
Mr Graves   Adolphus C. Dubois"

I forwarded the above to Mr Gamble with a note from myself intimating that I forgave him freely for all the unpleasantness to which I had been subject - and the subject dropped. Nothing more being heard of it. However, it can hardly be supposed that I quite recovered from the shock for some time afterwards - and how long the impression remained in the mind of the Secretary, or whether he really dispersed immediately all his unfavourable ideas respecting me I cannot say - but shortly afterwards he resigned his situation and left the Company's service.
==

Chapter 14th
In the summer of the year 1859 I and my wife went for an excursion to Granville on the coast of France, returning the same day. We went in the "Comête" steamer from Jersey together with about 60 others, and after a pleasant run of nearly three hours we arrived in safety but the weather was excessively warm that it was with difficulty we perambulated the town. The occasion was that of the "Fête Dieu" which amongst the Roman Catholiques is a very great day, the streets were hung with sheets on each sides, whilst a procession of priests & choristers walked through the town towards an altar which had been fitted up, covered with garlands of natural and artificial flowers of all sorts, candles, &c, &c. At this altar the procession halted and went through a rôle of religious performances usual on such occasions. As the Chef du Bureau Telegraphique was so kind as to permit me and my dear wife to view from his window the whole of the proceedings at the altar, we saw the whole splendidly - but in the eyes of Protestants such a mockery and idolatry were to a great extent quite disgusting. After the promenading was carried on throughout the town, the procession wended their way to the upper part of the town near the church overlooking the harbour and the sea - from this point the priest blessed the sea, invoking its aid for the increase in their commercial prosperity - this performance was accompanied by the firing of guns from the men-of-war in the harbour, at which time we embarked on board the steamer to return to Jersey - This was the only time I was ever on French soil, and the peculiarity of French manners as compared with the English was very striking. However we fared very well, at moderate prices, at the Hotel where we dined & as most of those who sat down could not speak French, the dinner scene was most amusing.

The Channel Islands' Telegraph Cable proved a most unfortunate one. Scarcely had the Company established themselves than breakdown commenced. By the numerous expensive operations of repairing the broken cable during the first and second year I obtained great experience in the practice of testing and repairing submarine cables and by dint of great perseverance endeavoured to improve myself in Electrical knowledge and to gain what information I could from every available source, resting well assured that it would be useful to me at some future time - thus I continued to work perseveringly in my business - endeavouring by all means to promote the interests of the Company, and to establish myself in the good opinions of those with whom I transacted business, as well as the other Island residents & natives - being persuaded that he who does to the utmost end himself for the welbeing of himself and his fellowmen, will meet with that Divine Assistance which will ultimately cause all things to work together for good; and this I have proved by experience, and I trust I am grateful for all the mercies which I have received from His hands.

In the month of September 1860 the Board of Trade made arrangements for the Establishment of a Meteorological Station at Jersey, with a view to warning the Seafaring population of approaching storms. After some correspondence instruments (Barometers and Thermometers) were forwarded to me and I was appointed agent for Jersey - and during the time the line of Telegraphic 'Communication' was intact I forwarded every morning a report by wire to the Board of Trade, which was with others published in the "Times", "Shipping Gazette" & "Globe" newspapers*. A little time afterwards "Signal Shapes" were furnished, and after some little trouble I made arrangements with the Lieut. Governor (Major Genl. Douglas) for the use of the signal staff at Fort Regent for hoisting signals when a gale was anticipated.

In the winter of 1860 I was requested by the Misses McNeill of Gorey, a fishing village in Jersey, to deliver a Lecture on the Electric Telegraph, in behalf of the Fisherman's Association at that Village, and to which I consented. On the 5th November I delivered the Lecture to a numerous audience who listened to the whole of it most attentively, and who were highly interested. This Lecture was published in the Jersey Independent Newspaper. The proceeds of the evening amounted to £15 which was to be appropriated to the extension of the Library of the Fisherman's Association, at the discretion of the Committee.

---

* Graves was paid 3/= (15p) per week by the Board of Trade for taking and transmitting the daily weather observations. [Eds]

Another addition was made to my family on December the 5th 1860 in the birth of a daughter whom we named Elizabeth Gooding* after the mother and sister of my wife.

The success of my Lecture at Gorey led speedily to numerous requests from other associations to lecture to their members. Amongst others there was a deputation from the "Working Man's Association" & also from the "Jersey Young Men's Christian Association" of which I was a member. Both of these required the lecture to be upon the "Electric Telegraph", but as the dates for their delivery came on two succeeding evenings, and as I had previously promised one to my own Association, I declined to lecture on that subject before the members of the former Society = but offered to do so on another subject, with which they were equally pleased. Accordingly on February 10 1861 I delivered one on "The Means of Acquiring Information" to the Working Men, being the same Lecture which I gave at Southampton, but slightly altered. This went off very satisfactorily, a complimentary vote of thanks being awarded me together with high eulogies upon the instructive Lecture I had given them. On the following evening I delivered the One on the "Electric Telegraph" to the Young Men's Christian Association". There were upwards of 300 persons, amongst whom were The Revd E. Heale, in the Chair, I. Rider Esqre, Jurat Neel, The Rev^d - Bull, The Rev^d - Murray, Mr Radford (of H.M. Customs), Mr Pattison & several other influential Gentlemen. The Lecture was illustrated by several different telegraphic Instruments - messages sent round the room, cannons fired by Electricity in illustration of blasting operations - and shocks were given to those who felt a desire to feel the effects of a battery. For several days afterwards I continued to receive congratulations of those who heard it, and several requested me to publish it in a pamphlet form, but I never did so, fearing to incur the displeasure of my Employers.

---

* who sadly died two years later while the family were based in London [Eds]

The morning after the delivery of this Lecture I was called to go to Guernsey to act as Electrician on board the Company's Steamship "Monarch" during the temporary absence of Mr G.E. Preece on a trial in London respecting the wilful injury of the Zandvoort and Dunwich Telegraph Cable whilst being laid, by a man in the employ of Messrs Newall & Co who had also obtained employment from the Contractors, the Complainants, Messrs Glass Elliott & Co. The Monarch at this time was engaged repairing the Channel Islands Cable between Alderney and Guernsey. During the time we were repairing this cable, I completed the manufacture of a Differential Galvanometer used for measuring distances of breaks in cables and both during these operations and ever after at Jersey all my tests and experiments were made with my own instrument.

[Editors' note]
The list of cable faults shown below has been taken from D. de Cogan: Annual Bulletin Société Jersiaise 27 (1998) 303 - 316

fault	Date	Location	Nature of fault	Duration
1	23 Nov. 1858	onshore	washed by sea	2 Days
2	26 Jan. 1859	off Jersey	abrasion	3 days
3	19 Apr.	off Portland	abrasion	26 days
4	17 Sept.	off Jersey	abrasion	19 days
5	1 Nov.	off Portland	abrasion	22 days
6	9 Jan. 1860	off Alderney	abrasion	26 days
7	25 Feb.	off Jersey	anchor damage	14 days
8	7 June	off Jersey	anchor damage	12 days
9	19 July	off Jersey	anchor damage	13 days
10	16 Sept.	off Alderney	abrasion	} 10
11	18 Sept.	off Jersey	anchor damage	} days
12	2 Jan. 1861	Jersey/Alderney	abrasion	55 days
13	28 March	Ald./W.mouth	abrasion	33 days
14	14 June	Ald./W.mouth	abandoned	

The constant and numerous failures of this line of telegraph especially between the islands, in consequence of the rocky nature of the bottom of the sea in those parts, gave rise to the following letter from the Board of Trade

Admiral FitzRoy at about the time of his correspondence with the author

> Board of Trade (and Admiralty)
> Meteorological Department
> 2 Parliament Street London
> 7   March 1861
>
> Sir
>
> I thank you for your obliging attention in sending Meteorological Notices of interest to this Office - all of which have been duly received. I regret that local difficulties near Jersey have compelled the Board of Trade to relinquish a Meteorological Station at that place where your cooperation has been so zealous and efficient:- and
>
>   I remain Sir,
>   Your obedient Servant
>
> Mr J. Graves   (signed) Robt FitzRoy
> Electric Telegraph Station
> Jersey"

I lost no time in replying to the above letter and represented why for several reasons Jersey should be retained as a "Signal Station" if not for an Observing Station" and requesting the Board to consider the matter.

On the fifteenth of March I was favoured with the following reply:-

> Sir,
> I acknowledge and thank you for your letter dated the 13th instant; -
> As your arguments and reasons seem sound and satisfactory - (assuredly not presumptuous) the Meteorological Department will include Jersey among the places to be warned - though Alderney will suit our purpose better for Meteorological Observations, and their transmission regularly to London.
> Will you therefore be good enough to retain the signals, now in your charge? and others shall be sent hence to Alderney -
> I am Sir, your obedient Servant
> (Signed) Robt FitzRoy

The author's copy of Admiral FitzRoy's signature (shown here) is extremely accurate [Eds]

Thus it will be seen that I succeeded in securing the establishment of a Storm Warning Signal Station at Jersey after the Board of Trade had relinquished their intention of doing so -
"

Daytime Signals

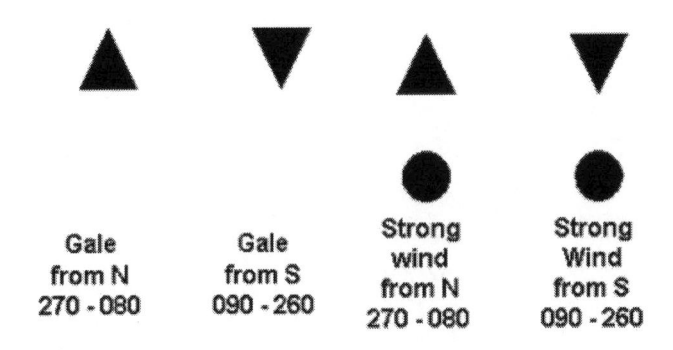

▲ ▼ ▲ ▼
　　　　● ●

| Gale from N 270 - 080 | Gale from S 090 - 260 | Strong wind from N 270 - 080 | Strong Wind from S 090 - 260 |

Night Signals

```
         RED        RED   RED          RED         RED   RED
  RED   RED         RED          RED   RED         RED

                                WHITE              WHITE

                                GREEN              GREEN
```

| Gale from N 270 - 080 | Gale from S 090 - 260 | Strong wind from N 270 - 080 | Strong Wind from S 090 - 260 |

Signals flow from Fort Regent when a storng wind or gale warning has been issued by JerseyMet.
Night signals are used in the daytime at Christmas and Easter.

Chapter 15th

The circumstance of my making the Electrical Instrument referred to in the last chapter, led to my appointment to the Company's steamship "Monarch" as Electrician, to superintend the repairs, and to test the electrical conditions of the various cables belonging to the Company as the Chief Engineer, C.F. Varley Esqre, afterwards informed me "for" said he, " a person who could without assistance, and with scanty means make an instrument of that description must have a good practical knowledge of the principles of the science, and therefore he considered that I was a fit person to fill the then existing vacancy.

Cableship *Monarch* during the laying of the Orford-Scheveningen cable

When this situation was at first offered me I doubted whether to accept it, as I was very comfortable at Jersey, but as the Channel Islands Telegraph Company appeared to be near its end, and in the last stage of consumption, I determined upon the advice of the Chief Engineer, to accept the certainty in preference to the uncertainty. Nevertheless, after having made so many friends in Jersey and having become so attached to the Island, I felt great reluctance to leave it - however, as the time approached for my departure, I addressed a farewell letter to the Editors of the Local Journals (with whom I had done a great deal of business in the supply of Telegraphic Intelligence) to which they gave publicity, adding their own comments thereon. The letter I sent them was as follows:-

>"St Helier's
>April 29. 1861
>
>Dear Sir,
>
>Having been appointed Electrician on board the Company's "Monarch" I regret to inform you that the natural consequences of the above appointment necessarily compel my departure from Jersey about the end of the present week. After having been connected with you and the Jersey public for nearly three years, it will be with a feeling of reluctance that I shall quit the shores of this picturesque Island. During my stay with you I have endeavoured to the best of my ability to give satisfaction to the public as well as to my employers; and how far I have succeeded in doing so, let public opinion decide.
>
>I am happy to say that I shall be succeeded by Mr G. Field, one of my early acquaintances in Telegraphic life, and one who I have reason to believe, will conscientiously discharge the duties imposed upon him.
>
>I regret that the Cable has during my sojourn here been so unfortunate; but when the history of telegraphic cables is thoroughly considered, it is a consolation to know that the Channel Islands Cable has not been the only one by far, which has suffered numerous disasters, whilst many have proved entire failures -
>
>Again expressing my regret at any separation from you
>
>I remain, Dear Sir,
>
>Yours faithfully
>
>To the Editor   James Graves"

Comments were published by the three local papers, The Jersey Independent, The Morning Express & The British Press in addition to the above letter:-

The British Press expressed its regret at my leaving the Island, and cordially wished me success wherever I might go. -

The Morning Express expressed itself in the following terms:- "The foregoing letter from Mr Graves will speak for itself. Suffice for us to say that a great loss will be felt by the people of Jersey on Mr Graves' departure. Though congratulating him on his new and important appointment we feel it our duty to express the many obligations we are under to that gentleman for his promptness, energy and tact displayed by him in the arduous duties of Manager of the Channel Islands' Electric Telegraph"

The "Jersey Independent" remarked:- "It will be seen from this letter that Mr James Graves, the respected local manager of the Channel Islands' Submarine Telegraph Company, is about to leave Jersey.

Assuming that Mr Graves' new employment is a step onward and upward in his profession, we congratulate him on his appointment. At the same time we must express the regret which we are sure will be widely felt at his separation from Jersey. During nearly three years that Mr Graves has been stationed in the Island, he has made numerous friends and we believe not a single enemy. In our relations with the Telegraph Office, we have always found Mr Graves untiring in his endeavours to give satisfaction, and most courteous and obliging in the discharge of his duties. In every way consistent with those duties Mr Graves has always been ready to give his assistance to every good movement having for its object the promotion of intellectual advancement and the general welfare; and we thing the friends of progress should pay him some compliment before his departure. Mr Graves has won private and public regard as much by his exemplary character as by his abilities and attainments which are of no ordinary degree.

We understand he is about to make Lowestoft his home, where he will carry with him the hearty good wishes of those (and they are not few) who esteem him as a man, a citizen and a friend."

Upon relinquishing my office of Meteorological Agent for the Board of Trade at Jersey and upon my offering to keep a record on board the "Monarch" I received the following complimentary note

> "Board of Trade (Meteorological Department)
> 2 Parliament Street, London S.W.
> 3rd May 1861.
>
> Sir,
> I regret to hear by your note of the 1st that we shall no longer have the benefit of your cooperation at Jersey. I thank you for your obliging offer to keep a Meteorological record while stationed on board the "Monarch" but on this occasion will not trouble you.
>
> I am Sir,
> Your obedient Servant
> (Signed) Robt. FitzRoy
>
> Mr. J. Graves
> Electric & International
> Telegraph Station
> Jersey

The foregoing complimentary reviews of my conduct and character during the two years and nine months that I was in Jersey must satisfy my readers that my efforts to give satisfaction to everyone were not in vain, but that, by God's assistance, I was enabled to keep such a line of conduct as should give satisfaction to all parties, and all opinions, whether commercial, political or religious, for as was justly remarked by the "Jersey Independent" I made numerous friends, but not to my knowledge, a single enemy, which was certainly remarkable, when the public position I held is duly taken into consideration. For these mercies the Lord be praised.

******** The manuscript ends at this point ********

Picture of staff at Foilhommerum Cliff, Valentia Island following the completion of the 1866 cable laying missions. It is believed that the author is the person with the white shirt in the centre. (From the Knight of Kerry's letter book in the IET Archives)

Printed in Poland
by Amazon Fulfillment
Poland Sp. z o.o., Wrocław